The Home Place

G.W. Zouck Publishing, LLC
Beckleysville, Maryland

Copyright © 2010 by Alathea Fisher Maxwell
Library of Congress Control Number: In Process
ISBN: 978-0-9817315-5-1

This book was set by PrintTech, Inc.
Book design by PrintTech, Inc
Cover design by Jennifer Marin Design

Printed in the United States of America
10 9 8 7 6 5 4 3 2 1

Acknowledgments

This book would never have been put together without the interest and encouragement of the following: My daughter, Cynthia Lee McDowell; my nieces Christine Alathea Martin & Bethany Martin Logan; and my great-niece, Alathea Widder Miutescu. Special thanks to the Holmes County Hub, which has printed my columns since 1972 and to my editor Emerson John Probst of G.W. Zouck Publishing who believes in my writings as a way of life.

-Alathea Maxwell

Table of contents

Prologue

Epilogue

Prologue

M y parents were Effie Brown Fisher and Herbert (Bert) Fisher. My Mama's family came to the north western part of what is now Holmes County, Ohio with other groups of settlers from the northwest corner of Virginia in the year 1811. Mama's paternal branch of the family had the distinction of being direct descendants of Daniel Boone's mother (before she was scalped following the birth of her 11th child). Her Mother's side of the family could claim a Revolutionary War patriot buried nearby. My Mother's parents had a lovely farm north of the little town of Nashville.

Papa's family settled in the same corner of Holmes County, after having traveled by covered wagon from Washington County Pennsylvania in 1843. My Papa's Grandpa Christian and Grandma Katherine Fisher rode in that small wagon with four young sons, one a baby on Katherine's lap. Those boys in that wagon would later fight for Holmes County in the Civil War. Three never came home, but the Fishers stayed on and my own Papa often remarked that he was the seventh son of the seventh son of those pioneers. The folklore of his Irish ancestors would call such a man gifted and whether he was or not, I thought he was the most wonderful man in all the world. His Papa, my dear Grandpa Fisher became a respected property owner in Nashville, and his brothers were stone masons and wagon makers that served the county.

Mama met Papa at a baseball game held in our small village one summer afternoon. After Bert hit a home run, had run the bases and was waving to the fans, he asked a teammate, "Who is the beautiful lady in the fourth row?" The friend replied, "She is the daughter of John and Marguerite Lee Brown, wealthy farmers who live north of Nashville." "Well," Bert said, "I'm going to marry her." Inquiring further, he learned that Miss Effie Brown was a graduate of the Ashland School of Music and taught piano to a loyal following of students from her small apartment in Ashland, a thriving town northwest of Nashville. Bert set out to court her.

Three weeks later they were engaged and planning their wedding. Such a stir it caused! The Brown's lovely daughter Effie was marrying Bert Fisher. So much to do and my Grandma Brown was so worried about a big wedding. Her health was not good but she didn't want to deny her daughter a beautiful day. A compromise was made, and instead of a big wedding at church, Mrs. Brown organized a lovely and intimate gathering at their home. The wedding included Effie's three brothers and her sister. The newlyweds spent their honeymoon in Effie's studio apartment in Ashland.

Herbert worked with his father, John, his brother Mike, and Bert's maternal uncle, Gil DeWitt, plastering the inside walls of new houses. There was no "drywall" in those days, instead all walls were added to the frame of a house in layers of wet plaster by hand trowel. Upon hearing that young men of his trade could find steady work thirty miles north in the city of Akron. Bert and Effie boarded the first train and stayed with his favorite cousin, Will Ridge, and wife, Mat.

Off Bert and Effie went to the employment office where Bert was assured of a steady job. They went house hunting and found a modest four bedroom home in a nice neighborhood. The next day they returned to Ashland and Effie began the emotional task of placing her many piano pupils with other teachers while Herbert began to pack her possessions in nice-sized wooden crates. Then, back to Nashville to say goodbyes to both sets of parents and families.

Driving up the long driveway of the farm, Effie noticed more horses and buggies than usual near the barn. She saw her father come out on the porch with some folks. They shaded their eyes as they looked her way. She saw the recognition in her father's eyes and held his gaze. Her heart sank. Effie had returned to her parent's home only to find that her mother had died that morning. First a wedding and now, a funeral. It was almost too much for Effie...now any children she might have would never know her wonderful mother. Her grief-stricken father wanted everything settled while they were all together. He and Marguerite had always planned to retire to the Rocky Mountains of Colorado...now he would go alone. Brother Walter wanted to continue farming at the family home. All Effie wanted was her mother. She settled for her mother's bed, dresser, corner cupboard, four kitchen chairs and, of course, her beloved piano.

When they returned to Akron, an exhausted Effie, a newlywed at 28 years old with the fresh loss of her beloved mother, and her new husband

(29) found a house that sparkled with cleanliness. Will and Mat Ridge had seen to everything possible.

Effie and Herbert had their first five children in their Akron home: John Lee, 1910; Alathea Kathryn (myself), 1911; Frances Estella, 1913; Helen May, 1916, and a tiny stillborn son, Ralph Edward in 1912; each one born in Grandma Brown's bed. Baby Helen was almost two when Herbert's father announced that new homes were being built back home in and around Nashville. There would be plenty of work for a plasterer. Would they like to come home and "rear" their children in their home town? The answer was "yes" and back to the hills and rolling countryside of Holmes County they went, where my childhood memories began.

Dedication

To my late brother, John Lee Fisher; my Mama, Effie Brown
Fisher; and my Papa, Herbert "Bert" Fisher

Childhood Memories

"There is nothing half so pleasant as coming home again."
—Margaret Elizabeth Sangster

Bidge. My First Friend

The house in which I was born had a small front yard and a sidewalk going to the front steps; on the porch were two rockers and a swing. The place was Akron, Ohio.

On the left side lived Mrs. Ertle and on the right, a woman, Mrs. Nevin, who had two children, Bidge and Sadie, the same age as John and me. All three houses were about the same and all were painted white. Landscaping consisted of a lilac bush and a Rose of Sharon. No fancy landscaping like today. The nice-sized backyards were as one so we children had lots of green space. On Mondays, which was wash day, the yards were off limits to us. They looked real pretty with all those lines holding clothes of different colors and sizes.

One Monday, John and I were in the Nevin house playing and eating cookies. When we decided to go home, Bidge wanted us to stay longer so he locked both doors and hid the keys. When his mother came to the back door with a basket of clothes, he had forgotten where he had hidden that key so she had to go around front. Bidge was not allowed to play until he found the other key. That night when Mrs. Nevin was playing the piano, the key fell out of her music.

One late afternoon when we were playing in the yards, Mrs. Nevin came out of our house and told us to get our nightclothes because we were going to stay at her house. "But it's supper time," I objected, "and Papa will soon be home." She told us that Mama wasn't feeling well and Mrs. Ertle called the doctor and he said she must go to bed and be very quiet. That night Mrs. Nevin went back over to our home and she stayed so long Mr. Nevin put us to bed. I thought it very strange—Mama had been sick before and there wasn't all this fuss.

The next morning Aunt Mat came and took us to her house for the day and when we got home that night, we ran upstairs to see Mama. She looked very tired and Papa was sitting by her bed. Mrs. Ertle came over with food. It wasn't until I was much older that Mama told me she had given birth to a baby boy who did not live, and she and Papa had named the baby boy Ralph Edward.

Coffee Soup

After Francie was born, Grandpa Fisher wanted Papa to come to Nashville because many new houses were being built and he needed him to help plaster inside walls. When we were already to move, Mrs. Nevin and Bidge and Sadie were so sad and Mrs. Ertle, who had no children, couldn't stop crying. It was hard to leave those friends and neighbors. Would we ever see them again?

When we did move, I was six, Francie four, and little Helen, two. All that I remember of the move were the tearful goodbyes.

Grandpa Fisher had three houses on Main Street and Mama was to have her pick. She chose the one that had a nice side yard and a barn at the rear. It was close to Grandma and Grandpa's, the grocery store, and not far from the school and the Methodist Church. It was the smallest of the three and Grandpa was surprised. Papa's brothers Mike and Martin lived near by and Mama's family a little farther outside of town on the Brown Family Farm.

We settled in and John and I met our teachers, Miss Mitten and Miss Jones. Papa and Grandpa had a new house south of Nashville to plaster and Mama found just the right corner for Grandma Brown's corner cupboard. We became acquainted with folks at church and Mama had some time to play the piano again. All was going well, and we enjoyed being near the families of our parents.

Then little Helen became ill. It appeared to be worse than a cold, so Doc Elder came to the house and soon told my parents the bad news: my baby sister had pneumonia. I have no idea what he did to care for her back then in 1917, but she got better and began to play with the doll Mama had made for her. However, one day when I was coming in the house from school, Doc Elder met me and said, "Helen now has double pneumonia and you must help your mother all you can." I was so frightened! First she had pneumonia and now she had "double pneumonia" so she must be twice as sick. I didn't understand then that it just meant "both lungs".

Papa and Grandpa moved Helen's bed to the kitchen because it was the largest and warmest room in the house. They then moved the couch from the living room to the kitchen for Mama. We learned to be very quiet during meals and to go elsewhere as much as possible. Grandpa came every afternoon and tried to get Mama to go out for some air, but she wouldn't do it. After several weeks, Helen began to smile and chatter, but then the fever again returned and the doctor told my parents the infection had returned and was worse. In spite of this, Doc Elder said "Effie, if you can get her to eat, I think we can pull her through."

Mama, so tired and sad, kept trying one thing after another. It didn't help any when Mama began blaming herself for Helen's illness, saying it was because she chose "this drafty old house."

I followed the doctor and Papa to the door one night and soon after, I heard Doc Elder say "Bert, you are going to have to quit working for awhile. Effie is taking care of Helen but you are going to have to take care of Effie." Papa nodded thoughtfully and after that, made Mama go to bed every afternoon and take a long nap. Oh, our house was so gloomy with Mama so tired and sad. None of us smiled anymore.

One evening Papa made Mama her favorite snack: a cup of coffee with lots of cream and a slice of bread spread with butter and sugar. She dipped the bread into her cup of coffee as baby Helen watched. Papa noticed and put his hand on the crook of Mama's arm. As Mama began to eat, Helen surprised us all and said, "Me!" Mama gave Helen a tiny bite, sweet with sugar and soaked in coffee. She wanted more! Papa ran out the door to Doc Elder's and when they both returned Doc said, "Well, I'll be doggoned...poor little girl is going to get well on coffee soup."

Helen had to learn to walk again and her thick brown hair changed color. At first, it turned white, then later, a dark fuzzy brown, and finally, as Mama described it, "the color of a young chestnut before it hit the ground." How happy we were to have our darling baby sister chattering after us and getting into things again. Mama and Papa let Helen eat coffee soup every morning until she was six years old.

Crying Time

Children react differently to the same situation—some pout or get angry, others refuse to talk and some cry. I was the crying type. A change in routine caused my first outburst.

First grade began in a city school and ended in a country school. The first half of the year I entered my large classroom in Akron, Ohio, and each morning the teacher greeted us at the door. We were expected to say, "Good morning, teacher," then as we walked in front of her, we would say, "Excuse me, teacher." She was strict about having good manners. When my parents decided to return to their familiar home town to be nearer my grandparents, I entered a new school that was quite small. Although a nice brick building, it stood in the middle of a corn field set back from the main road that traveled east to west through that little town. When I entered the school room, all eyes were on me. I took a deep breath, and since there was no teacher standing at the door I walked over to her desk and said, "Good morning, teacher." A boy in the front row looked me up and down and said, "Because you are new here, you are trying to be teacher's pet." I burst into tears – just an awful way to begin my first day.

The next day it happened again – the tears, I mean. I was busy at my desk coloring a picture eager to show my new classmates that even though I came from a different school, I still knew how to color. When I am really engrossed, I have a tendency to "work" my mouth. I saw Miss Jones watching me, and thinking she was impressed by my coloring, I pressed on deep in concentration. Miss Jones said, "Alathea, spit out your gum."

I blinked, "I...I...I am not chewing gum." I replied unsteadily, looking around at my classmates. There weren't very many happy first grade faces looking back at me.

"Well, then," she said, "you swallowed it." and made me sit in a chair at the front of the room. I tried to explain because she seemed like a nice teacher, but she did not believe me and I cried because she thought I lied.

The next day I kept my eyes down and didn't talk very much. When it came time to color, I forgot my troubles and again concentrated on the task before me. I happened to look up and Miss Jones was staring straight at me. "Oh no," I thought with dread. And then she told the class she owed me an apology because she was sure I had been telling the truth about not having any gum, and I cried again because she knew I did not lie.

In the second grade I had another crying time. I walked to school each day with a girl who always put her arm around my shoulder and her hand felt like a brick. When I told her my shoulder hurt, she simply walked around me and hung on my other side. I was real proud of myself when, instead of crying, I said firmly, "Stop it!" She stared at me with open mouth and then knocked the book from my hand. When I stooped to pick it up, the cover was wet with tears.

Posy Room

It was a small room but large enough to hold a bed, a dresser, and a rocker that had been Grandma Brown's. A rag rug from Aunt Della covered the floor. I called it the *Posy Room* because the wallpaper had lots of flowers.

During the warmer months, Mama did all her cooking, baking, and preserving in the summer kitchen, a large, airy room with windows that could open to let the light in and the hot air out. The *Posy Room* was located just off the dining room but in winter, the dining room became the kitchen because it was too difficult to heat the summer kitchen. Uncle Gil and Uncle Mike would help Papa move the sideboard into the hall so the room had space for the stove. Linoleum covered the floors so it was an easy transition from that point of view and the furniture could glide right across the room. Mama put rag rugs over the open spaces and we had a cozy, warm kitchen.

It was unfortunate that Francie became sick that winter because she could smell the food when she didn't have an appetite. It was the first day of holiday vacation and Francie came into the kitchen looking like a ripe strawberry with a forehead as hot as the top of the cook stove. Mama quickly put her to bed in the *Posy Room* and told John (10), Helen (4) and me (9) to stay away from her while she walked uptown to get Doctor Elder.

After Doc Elder took a look at Francie he walked into the make-shift kitchen and said, "Effie, its scarlet fever. She must not leave her room until I return in a week. Always keep her door closed and, for double protection, hang a blanket on this side. You must always wash your hands because it is so contagious. The other children may not leave the house."

It was his last remark that brought forth tears and choruses of dismay. There were two sledding parties coming up in town and Uncle Walter Brown had planned a sleigh-riding party for all the small cousins. We simply could NOT miss that. As it turned out, that didn't matter for not so much as a flake fell all during the holidays.

So there we were. Only the kitchen and living room were heated and getting to the living room meant going through the hall, which was as cold as outside. Those first days were awful. Francie was pretty sick and John and I played enough Parcheesi to last a lifetime. Mama had two card games, *Authors* and *Musicians*, and we played them over and over. Each card would list the name of the author (or musician), their likeness, and their writings or compositions. I still have both decks and whether or not the illustrations depicted the true likeliness of each famous individual, I will forever hold those images in my head. My favorite, of course, was the female author Louisa May Alcott. Mama was so busy with Francie we scarcely knew she was around.

When Francie was getting better, she was always calling for us so we sat on the floor outside her door and talked back and forth. We made up stories and asked her questions such as, "Are you still red? Are you hungry? How many flowers are there on the wallpaper above your bed? What boy do you like in your class?" on and on and on. Each time Francie would say her answers as loudly as she dared so we could hear her through the door and the blanket. Sometimes, we would tease her for a spell by talking just loud enough for her to hear that someone was on the other side of the door. "What are you talking about?" she would cry.

One day, she had a crying spell and Mama asked John, Helen, and me to put on warm clothes and go outdoors to look in her window where she could easily see us. We would make faces at each other and one time, John got one of the chickens and held it up to the window standing beneath it out of sight and making "chicken talk" so Francie could have a chat with someone "new." Dear John. He then went to the barn and got old Mollie out of her stall and led her to the window so Francie could have a look. Mama played and played the piano during that time. We thought surely it was to entertain us but looking back I imagine it was to block out our noise.

At last the week was over and in came the doctor. "My, my…you're all doing just fine. How about you, Effie, are you all worn out?" He granted Francie leave to play with her siblings and instructed Mama to give the *Posy Room* a good scrubbing. We had one week of vacation left and now we could walk uptown, however Francie had to stay inside for another week, exclaiming, "At least I'm out of jail!"

Doc Elder and Mama sat in the kitchen over cups of coffee and from out of the murmur of their conversation I heard Doc say, "It's too bad Bert has to be working in Florida weeks on end." Mama reminded Doc that no homes were built in Ohio during the winter months when it was too cold to plaster. Papa had to go to Florida to plaster houses there until springtime came. I often wondered what all Mama wrote in her letters to Papa. Did she miss him? Certainly with all us children to keep her company she didn't have time to worry about Papa. She would have had lots to say but one thing I do know: that was the only case of scarlet fever in our house that year.

Saturday Nights

In the early 1900s, Saturday night was the best night in the week for the Fisher family of Nashville, Ohio. It all began with a bath, then supper, and ended with a party up town. Since Nashville had no running water at that time, we only washed up during the week and had a real bath on Saturday night. Mama went out the back door of the kitchen and took the wash tub off a big hook on the wall. In the summer, she would put the tub in the kitchen by the side door because it was closest to the outside pump. She then fetched and carried several buckets of water up two steps into the house and poured them in the tub. She kept kettles of water boiling on the stove to add to the water as needed.

While little Helen was being bathed in the tub, Francie and I, who had been playing outside in our bare feet, had to first wash up in the big ceramic bowl that rested on a stand in the corner of the kitchen. Mama had made a pretty skirt that wrapped around the top of the wash stand and on a shelf below were towels and washcloths. By the time it was my turn to step into the bathwater used by my younger sisters, Mama had added more hot water from the stove. Ahhhhh…it felt so good. What a delight to be in the water and have a chance to splash at each other. With a smile on her face, Mama busied herself mopping up the water on the linoleum of the kitchen floor.

Finally, we girls were sent upstairs to dress and it was my brother John's turn in the washtub. After all were clean, John and I filled the buckets back up with tub water, and passed them to Mama who poured the soapy water on our Golden Glow bush by the kitchen door. We were thanked for this effort with bursting blooms of golden blossoms all summer. Bath day over, Mama sat to rest a bit as it was not an easy task. Was it any wonder why we only did that once a week? It was a miracle for all of us when our little town got running water and it came inside our house!

In spite of all the work that was done that day, Mama called it her *day off* because our typical Saturday supper was friend potatoes, eggs and applesauce washed down with a cold, cold glass of milk brought up from the cellar. By early evening, we were ready for the best part of all…the party.

With happiness floating around our family we started walking up the hill, Papa carrying Helen, Mama holding Francie by the hand and John and I racing to the top. We took the dirt path most of the way for about three quarters of a mile. Folks that lived near the path would pour cinders from their coal stoves on the path in rainy weather so passers-by wouldn't have to deal with too much mud. When we reached Main Street we had a sidewalk even though Main Street was still a dirt road through town*. We passed Doc Elder's home and the little telephone office and then on to the Bittner's General Store. Entering through the front we walked through the shelves of groceries to the small room in the back where we had our party.

---

* A few years later, big machines came in to town to pave Main Street. Francie was the talk of the town because she sat on the curb by the General Store with her chin in her hands and intently watched those machines pave that road. She sat there every day and whenever it was time for supper either John or I had to run all the way up the hill and then up to Main Street to make her come home. They paved both lanes of the street through town and once they came to the end they paved only one side of the road all the way west to the next town. If you intended to pass someone on that road, you had to go off on the dirt.

Our parents' friends were waiting with their four children. We children were to have our own table! But first, we went to the counter and the jolly store owner began putting ice cream in eight small square cardboard dishes. Ice cream was what this party was all about. Back at our table we savored it, rolling our eyes to the heavens, took our time, and ate ever so slowly. With the last bite in our mouths our parents, who had been sitting together amongst laughter and chatter would call out (just as we knew they would) "Harry, give the kids seconds". Delighted, we trooped back to the counter with our cardboard dishes and Harry filled them up.

More fun was to come as Papa's friend got out his harmonica and Papa began clog dancing. He was so good at it that people who would happen into the grocery store would say, "Do it again, Bert." At this point, everyone was getting pretty noisy and before we knew it the party was over until the next Saturday night. We walked home before dark the same way we had arrived with baby in Papa's arms and John and I running. We were allowed one game of Parcheesi and off to bed. Yes, Saturday nights in Nashville long ago were special…very special indeed.

Francie Sings

The hill that led to my childhood home contained a wide lane that belonged to the village but was not a through road for traffic and remains so today. We were very much by ourselves. Our yard was so long and wide that by the time my brother John got it mowed with the circular tines of the rotary push mower, it was time to start over. One week John sprained his ankle playing ball and our father had to take over the chore of pushing the mower. After a long day of mowing, Dad decided the lawn should end just beyond the coal shed and the rest become a field. In no time at all we kids had made a footpath through the field because Aunt Reed lived at the other end. She was alone and Mama was always sending her food because, as she said, "It is hard for Aunt Reed to cook beef and noodles or bake pie when she doesn't have a husband."

The spring of 1919 was beautiful—just the way it was supposed to be. The spicy fragrance of the clove bush on the east side of the house filled the entire yard. Jars of seeds gathered the year before sat neatly in a row on a bench in the cool summer kitchen, waiting to be planted. We kept telling Mama it was time to go barefoot.

One end of the long kitchen table served as a desk for Mama. She separated the space by lining up her mother's many china tea pots across the width of the table. We were not to go past those teapots! She was busy on that June afternoon sorting material for Children's Day at the Methodist Church in our small village of Nashville, Ohio. My sister Francie and I always sang a duet—she, alto, I, soprano. The songs, some of which I still have, were witty and lively and we loved singing them.

Our new summer dresses were made especially for that momentous day and that year they were of white voile with short front panels and trimmed in lace. Children's Day arrived as a lovely sunny morning and we went through the usual rush with four children to get ready for church.

When we arrived at the church door, Francie suddenly became stubborn, stomped her feet and said she had decided not to sing and she was going home. There was no point in coaxing her and Mama, holding the youngest on her hip and herding my brother and me sighed and said I would have to sing alone. I was not happy about that. Not…at…all.

The church was packed and we tried to be at ease in our chairs on the stage. Some of the kids asked, "Where's Francie?" but a teacher said, "shhhhh." Soon it was my turn and just as Mama was saying that I would be singing alone because…the door of the church opened and Francie walked up the aisle as big as you please, came up onto the stage, took her place beside me, nodded, and proceeded to sing the duet with me. She then exited by taking the three steps down from the stage in one jump and strode back down the aisle and out through the two big front doors. There was so much clapping and laughter that we never noticed our baby sister, little Helen, toddling behind her. Mama went to the front of the stage and said directly to my disgusted eleven year old brother who was in the audience, "John, you had better go with your sisters."

When Mama and I arrived home, Francie, still in her good dress, was sitting on the platform that held the water pump, giving Virgie the cat a bath. Helen, all eyes, was sitting on the kitchen steps, her pretty new shoes all splashed with water. After a good scolding from Mother, Francie said with an impish grin, "I sang, didn't I?" The look on my brother John's face indicated he had just plain given up on those two girls.

By this time, we were late for dinner at Grandma's house. Papa was to meet us there because he'd gone to Grandma's early since he was "not a church-going person." Before long, he came looking for us as we made our way there. We had a good laugh as we told the story of Francie singing in church. Papa remarked that perhaps it might be kind of interesting going to church after all. After he died years later, we found in his wallet a small, worn, creased picture of Jesus and a Bible verse beneath it signed, "Love, Effie" —a token to him from our mother.

Rain on Washday

During my childhood I had a skeptical attitude about rain-filled clouds. A driving summer rain forced us to play indoors and we sat at the kitchen table arguing over a game of Parcheesi or curled up someplace rereading books by Zane Grey and Louisa May Alcott. Mama would play the piano and we would sing patriotic songs. However, we considered these to be night time activities and preferred to be outside playing during the day. Except when it rained.

The happiest days consisted of playing ball or hide and seek, running in the fields and wading in the creek. A sudden downpour could change the day. Rain often sent a wet and smelly cocker spaniel rushing into the house and one of us had the unpleasant task of drying her. Siblings, who otherwise were the best of friends, became irritable with one another. Rain on a Monday, the standard washday in northeastern Ohio in those days, could spoil my mother's plans for an entire week. The first thing she did on Monday was to look at the sky. Rarely did she misjudge the weather.

Mama had been advised by the doctor to slow down a little and to have help with the laundry. Instead of hiring help, which was unaffordable, she walked to our school, spoke with the superintendant and made arrangements that I would help with laundry one Monday, and my brother the next.

On "my" Monday I ran to school after Mama and I had gotten all the clothes hung on the clothesline. As the afternoon wore on, sitting in my grade school classroom, I followed a bright ray of sunshine coming through the window that danced across the blackboard, daydreaming about all those clothes flapping in the warm breeze.

Suddenly, the bright spot of sun vanished and the room became somber and mysterious. Over the tops of her glasses Miss Bell looked at me and said "A storm is coming. You should run home and get the wash off the line before it arrives."

I ran out the front door of the school and along the dirt Main Street perhaps a half mile. Still running as fast as I could, I veered left at our street, another half mile and down the hill to home. I knew the clothes must be dry by now but if they got wet, it would mean hanging them up all over again in the summer kitchen. At top speed I crossed the yard, grabbed the clothespin bag from the basket, put it around my neck and started yanking clothes off the line pell-mell.

With one eye on the sky I took the time to fold the clothes and then stooped to gather the stray clothespins. The sky was one big black cloud as I rushed up the steps to the kitchen with the basket of sweet-smelling clothes. Holding the screen door open with one hand, I lugged the basket up with the other. Mama was taking her required nap and I piled the clothes by the kitchen table where she would sprinkle them with water to dampen them before ironing.

My heart was pounding with excitement—what fun playing games with the clouds. I cut a thick slice of bread, dabbed it with apple butter, hurried up the hill, took the back road to school and reached the entry as thunder rumbled around the building. Plop…plop…big rain drops hit the warm stone steps of the school, bringing with them the scent of the first warm rain drops mixing with dust. By the time I reached the classroom, I could see sheets of rain from the first spring storm soaking the ground.

I was overflowing with joy. I had been victorious in a race with the weather. Never before had I felt so alive! I was conscious of a deep down feeling of elation and satisfaction. I had walked to school after an early morning of washing clothes, ran all the way home to help my Mama and beat the rain and walked back to school before she awoke from her nap. How wonderful to have such a day of suspense and be only eight years old. At that moment I didn't really care if I ever grew up. The present was good enough. I was a winner….let it rain.

"Across the windowpane it pours and pours

and swift and wide with a muddy tide,

Like a river down the gutter roars

The rain, the welcome rain!"

- Longfellow

Miss Bell

The end of the school year grew near. At that time, there were two grades in each room. My sister Francie was in first grade, I was in second. At the end of the year, Miss Mitten got the not-so-bright idea that it would be chummy if she held me back a year so we two sisters could graduate together. She talked this over with Mama who, to our surprise, approved. My sister and I hated it. She didn't like to study and I was a little bookworm. Furthermore, she had her friends; I had mine. But worst of all, other students thought I had failed.

Then along came Miss Bell who had taught school for many years and would now teach the third and fourth grade. She rented the front parlor at my Grandmother's house and I loved what she did with it. Her couch, with a pretty cover and cushions, became her bed at night. There was a beautiful old desk, a bookcase with five shelves, lovely tables and lamps. We became good friends and I can still picture us sitting there listening to Victrola records, her gray hair pulled back into a thin bun and mine in pigtails.

One day I recited all ten versus of my favorite poem, *The Children's Hour* by H.W. Longfellow: "Between the dark and the daylight, when the night is beginning to lower, comes a pause in the day's occupations that is known as the children's hour…" I can still see her look of astonishment. I told her I should really be entering fourth grade, and not the third, and told her the rest. After hearing my sad lament she said thoughtfully, "That was not a wise decision and so unfair to you."

During those lazy summer days, Miss Bell asked me to learn the multiplication tables forward and backwards and in-between. While she sat in a straight-backed chair, enjoying the shade in the grape arbor, I chanted them for her, over and over…six times eight is forty-eight…eight times eight is sixty-four. August came and soon we were back in school on a hot autumn day. My sister and I entered the third grade…together. On the second day of school, I couldn't believe it when Miss Bell made an announcement. "Can anyone in this class recite the multiplication tables without making a mistake?" I held up my hand, she nodded her assent, and I blew through them like a breeze. Miss Bell said, "Please pick up your books and move to a fourth grade desk."

After school I ran to Grandma's house and waited for my understanding teacher. When she arrived, I put my arms around her waist and exclaimed with childish exuberance, "Miss Bell, I love you, I love you, I love you!" At first, I thought she was going to hug me and I hoped that she would because she needed someone to love, but she patted me rather awkwardly and said, "Now, now child, run along and play."

Sometime later down the road, Miss Mitten and my mother agreed they had made a mistake. To her credit, Miss Mitten agreed, "Miss Bell came along at just the right time".

When school bells summon children back to school a strange yet familiar silence hovers over the neighborhood. The basketball net looks forlorn, no one is in the baseball field, and the trampoline waits for jumping feet. The absence of childish laughter and happy voices make the afternoon hours seem somber. School begins when the joe pye weed that has livened the landscape with its deep rose flowers becomes less conspicuous and their color is replaced by the lush yellows of the golden rod; the last golden breath of the summer sun.

The end of summer often causes disquietude and although we grow accustomed to the stillness it still leaves a reminder of another summer gone. With its end a poem entitled *End of August...* "Summer is losing some of its wattage; pipes are oozing down at the cottage. Golf greens are browning, baseball is pallid, nobody's downing potato salad. Kids are despairing but all the while, Mothers are wearing the ghost of a smile."

Nine Lives

It had been a hot summer but on that night back in the early twenties, a gentle breeze rustled the curtains in the open windows. It was four in the morning when I was awakened from a sound sleep by piano music coming from downstairs. Surely Mama wasn't playing at this hour. I stayed in bed until I was fully awake...yes...I heard it ...a constant trilling of the piano keys. Frightened, I ran into my parents' room and shaking Mama none too gently, I said, "Someone is playing our piano."

When Papa told me my imagination was running rampant, I insisted, "Listen!" Mama jumped out of bed and said, "That means bad luck in the family!" Joined by three siblings my parents and I sneaked down the stairs as quietly as we could into the living room and there before our eyes, in the moonlight streaming through the window, was a cat running up and down the keyboard. Hmmmmm…we never had a cat in our house. Not ever. Strict orders kept our barn cats in the BARN.

Papa looked skeptically at Francie, who kept her eyes on the floor while she quickly scooped up Virgie the cat (named after a favorite Aunt). I saw Mama standing there smiling at the six of us in the middle of the living room in our nightclothes. Papa saw no humor in the tableau. On the first cool night in six weeks he had been awakened at four in the morning because of a silly barn cat that Francie, always the animal lover, had hidden in her room. "Fetch the lantern and get that cat back to the barn," Papa instructed Francie, who did as she was told. My brother and I exchanged looks and we went back upstairs to bed.

What Papa didn't know was that earlier that day as John and I were working in the garden, Francie had come running, "Come quick! Virgie is having kittens in the hay mow!" John, always the nine year-old man in charge said, "So what?!" I wanted to see those babies but I thought John knew everything and since he didn't care, well, neither would I. Those kittens became the center of my sister's life and she took complete care of them until they were raised.

All went smoothly until Aunt Mat came for a visit. The kittens were about three weeks old and Francie had placed them in the folds of the old davenport cushion. Aunt Mat walked in the living room and sat down… almost, but not quite…on the little mound of fur. We screamed, "Don't sit there!" and poor Aunt Mat, scared out of her wits, slid gently off the cushion and right to the floor. She was a large woman and it took all of us to get her up. "Oh please, puhleeeeese, don't tell Mama and Papa (who were out in the garden) that you fell!" Aunt Mat gave us all a scowl and then grinned and replied, "I've never tattled on anyone in my life!" We smothered her with kisses.

Some days later, Francie apparently decided that Mama Cat looked worn out, so she smuggled her to the most comfortable place in the house, our parent's bed. After making Virgie all nice and comfy in the down, Francie came outside in search of me. "Come and see!" she said. By the time we got back upstairs, Virgie had become entangled in the silky fringe that edged the pretty throw Mama always spread out over the pillows. To make matters worse, we knew that throw had belonged to Mama's mother, our Grandma Brown who had died while Mama and Papa were on their honeymoon. We never even got to meet her.

This was something Francie could not hide and she yelled for Mama, who came rushing upstairs, took one look, picked up that cat amidst great protestations, raised the window and tossed that cat out to the ground. We screamed, "Virgie!"

"Oh hush," Mama said, "a cat has nine lives," and the all-knowing John who had entered the room remarked, "One down and eight to go." We rushed to the window just in time to see Virgie shake herself off with great indignance and trot towards the barn.

My sister brought every manner of fur and fowl into our house as she was growing up. Baby birds who had fallen out of the nest, bunnies that were no bigger than our fist that she would find just as it was getting dark at the end of our yard. Kittens, puppies, a rooster with a broken leg, and once she found the worst scraggly tom cat you ever saw. Those that lived always ended up in the barn because we couldn't get anything past our Mama. But Francie, who never had children after she was grown and married, adopted homeless animals for the rest of her life.

Amy Hilda

It was mid-summer of 1920—the sun was shining, birds singing, baseball in full swing in the field, flowers blooming around the side porch, but none of this mattered because Mama was ill. Papa had his brother Uncle Mike come from his log cabin to help move a bed downstairs. Then he went to Big Prairie to get his sister, our Aunt Cora.

We asked Doc Elder what was wrong with Mama. He told us she was going to have a baby and since she was 40 and already mother of four children, she must spend some time in bed. Mama, in her nightgown and kimono, smiled and said, "Don't look so worried – it will be such fun having a baby in the house." We were not the least bit curious as to how the baby would get there. That is how it was in the 1920's.

Aunt Cora came and brought our first meal in her own favorite kettle. She also brought her special fudge recipe. The next morning Papa and Grandpa Fisher went to plaster a house a short distance to the South in the beautiful hills of Glenmont. On arriving home, Papa found Doc Elder telling Mama her father, who had retired to Colorado, had died and she must not go to the funeral even though it would be in Nashville. This was very sad for Mama, she had lost her mother the year she married Papa, and now her father just when the new baby was due to arrive.

That night Mama didn't want to eat supper with us; Aunt Cora gave me a nice white cloth to place on Mama's forehead. I knew it was one of Grandma Brown's dinner napkins because it had an embroidered "B" on the edge. Mama moaned off and on and Papa made us go to bed early and he said very sternly, "No talking or running around—go right to sleep."

The next morning I hurried downstairs. Aunt Cora was rushing here and there and Doc Elder was just leaving. Papa said, "Come and see your baby sister, Amy Hilda." She was sound asleep and Mama was very tired. I ran back upstairs, "Get awake everybody – there's a baby in bed with Mama."

Amy Hilda (pronounced Ammie with a soft "a") became the center of our lives. Francie would sit by her crib waiting for her to get awake. When she began crawling, little Helen would crawl beside her. Each morning when we heard her first cry, we all dashed upstairs—John and I always argued over who could carry her down so Mama made us take turns.

Aunt Cora stayed for several more weeks and it's a good thing she did because on October 23, our beloved Grandpa Fisher was coming up from the cellar and had a heart attack and died. He fell face down, on the hard ground. I was so sad, and Amy Hilda would never really know him.

The year flew by and Amy, going on two, had learned to walk. She was the happiest child and when Mama told her we would soon be coming home from school, she would pull her little chair to the door and sit there waiting. Then came a day when Amy wasn't there—she had developed a high fever and Mama was sitting in the rocker near the stove holding Amy close to her breaking heart. The doctor told her Amy had pneumonia.

The next morning Amy was gone. For days and days someone was crying. Then one morning I heard Mama trying to whistle but her eyes were filled with tears. Halfway up the hill to school I turned and went back home. As I entered the door I heard Mama crying; her sobbing was so intense it frightened me. I went into the *Posey Room*, put my arms around her and she said, "Oh, why did you come back?" I went to the dresser and got her mother's dinner napkin and she pressed it close to her face. I said, "Mama, it's such lovely day, walk up the hill with me." When we reached the top, our neighbor Mrs. Drake came out and said, "Effie, come up and have some coffee." After hesitating, Mama went up the steps to her neighbor's warm embrace.

I went on to school feeling a twinge of happiness. I was only nine but I knew no matter what the day might bring, Mama's morning was spent with a friend.

The Flower Garden

The dirt path went weaving by the outside cellar door, past the downstairs bedroom where my mother often rested, twisted by the thorny fire bush, hurried down a slope, took a sharp turn to the right around the chicken yard and to the door of the unpainted barn. It then led past the stalls of horses, with Mollie and Duke, to the rear door where there was only one step when there should have been three.

My brother and I stood in this doorway one raw spring day looking down at what had once been used as a pig sty by a former owner. The area was fenced in with wide, weather-beaten boards. "Do you know what, Sis—this would make a nice flower garden." Since both of us were blessed with a vision to see how something ugly could become something beautiful, I agreed without hesitation.

That night John sat at the kitchen table sketching plans as to how he wanted the flower beds to look. Mama, who always planted zinnias and marigolds around the vegetable garden, said we could have some of the seeds she saved and she named other annuals we knew nothing about. John and I decided to pool our pennies to buy some of the flowers mother described in such glowing terms.

The next morning John began spading and I raked and piled the stones. "Well," my brother said, "the yellow bed is done, now let's start on the red one." He knew exactly where he was going to plant each seed.

It was difficult to be patient while waiting for the seeds to sprout and when they started peeking at us, we didn't give weeds a chance to grow. We were always scanning the sky hoping for rain or wishing it wouldn't rain so much. I don't remember our talking about goals in life – this one goal was enough since John was just thirteen and I was eleven.

When the first buds appeared, we counted them—there were 200 and we couldn't believe our good fortune. When the first marigold opened its yellow, fluffy head, John beat me to the garden – it was early morning and I ran down in my nightclothes. The grass felt cool and I decided the nicest time of day was before the hot sun blazed across the earth.

It became an evening ritual for the family to visit our haven. None of us knew we had planted typical old-fashioned flower beds that would one day be seen in a restored Williamsburg. "You know," John said, "I wouldn't change a thing—like the cosmos in the four corners and the morning glories make you want to get up early to see them at their best."

For two seasons we had our flowers and then John got a part-time job and was on the baseball team and all sorts of things got in the way. At the end of the second season, and after the first frost with only minutes before night would fall, I, a lonely thirteen-year-old, stood for the last time in the barn doorway and looked down at, what was now, an area of dirt. A few annuals still stood wearily on their feet and rotting string held some grasping brown vines.

It was an oppressive moment for one so young to realize there would never be another spring like the one before. It had all been such fun but without my brother, the excitement would be gone. I wondered if life would be happiness and sorrow all mixed together. I could not understand my deep down sadness—I needed to talk to someone.

I remember—oh, how well I remember, how grateful I was to have in my little world, an understanding mother who enclosed me with her arms. "Next spring," she said, "you and I shall have a flower bed by the back porch and around the pump. Yellow will be our main color—how pretty from the kitchen window…."

As the evening came and my mother was framed in the back light of the kitchen window, I admired her profile. Some wisps of her brown hair had come lose from the braids wrapped around her head, and they fluttered in the breeze. And there, in the dimness of twilight and feeling the first breath of winter, all I could think of was spring.

Jealousy

Most of us go through a period of instinctive envy or jealousy. I didn't grow out of it until envy and jealousy made me almost sick a few times. I had to stop indulging myself unless I wanted those two destructive emotions to eat me alive.

I know why I clipped that from a magazine so many years ago. It was because it applied to me. Permit me tell you of three occasions. I was about ten when a new little girl from the city moved to our little town. I resented her from the beginning. Although Mama, an expert seamstress, made our beautiful dresses from *Ladies' Home Journal* patterns, Jane had a city look and city ways. Mother told me I was missing an opportunity to make a new friend because of my jealousy. I knew she was right and I didn't feel good about it. She lived there only two years and I really did try to be nice, but I never quite succeeded.

Another time, due to the fact we often needed another bed for relatives, we had, in our living room, a day bed instead of a davenport. It had a nice cover and an abundance of pillows Mama made, but I envied my friends who had davenports. Then Aunt Mat came for the night and I heard her tell Mama she had never seen such beautiful cushions. "Effie," she said, "you could sell those in a city store." I then looked at it differently—so that took care of that gnawing bit of envy.

The third time marked the beginning of a new life for me. I was thirteen when Mama was planning her annual piano recital which always filled the Methodist Church. Each pupil was given two pieces to learn and would then play the one she did best. Ruth and I loved the same piece so Mama said we should both practice hard and the one who performed it best would play it that special night.

As it turned out, I had to agree with Mama that Ruth played it with much more expression than I. As the night drew near, I was hoping Ruth would get sick, not awful sick, but bad enough to keep her from the recital. Fate was cruel when on that auspicious day, Ruth did become ill. Not only did she become ill but she later died. I was crushed and refused to play her music. In fact, I never wanted to play the piano again.

That night I began crying; the next day I wouldn't eat breakfast and I refused to go to school. Mama thought I was just sad, but I then got sick to my stomach and developed a fever. The doctor said he could find nothing wrong.

I finally broke down and between sobs told Mama it was my fault Ruth had died—God misunderstood me. Mama then told me Ruth had a very bad heart and had not been expected to live that long. "Didn't you notice Ruth was always reading or practicing?" she asked.

A great load had been lifted from me and I solemnly promised myself to never, ever be jealous again. It truly was a green-eyed monster.

I also learned that envy can be a good thing if it stimulates people to do better. "You can be somebody with a plan of your own; you can say no and you won't be alone. You can make yourself higher than you have ever known, by making up your mind, doing things your own way, setting up your own style, by being yourself." – Anonymous

The End of Crying Times

I was 12 years old when I had my last childish crying spell. It was hunting season and Papa's friend, Charlie, came from the nearby city of Canton to spend the day. After an early supper, Papa went outside to do chores and Charlie sat in the kitchen rocker smoking a cigar while I cleared the table for Mama.

As I passed Charlie, he pulled on my arm and said, "Come and sit on old Charlie's lap." Now, let me tell you I hate cigars and I was too big to sit on the lap of my father's friend, so I pulled away. He reached out once more and a few tears escaped. Mama turned away from the dishpan and told Charlie to stop teasing. Papa had just entered the room and he and Mama exchanged glances after which Papa said, "Charlie, I think your hunting day is over." Charlie replied with surprise, "Bert, you know I love your kids," and Papa answered, "She's not a kid," and opened the door.

I felt confused—all this because I was crying? Then Papa said, "Sometimes it's better to get mad than it is to cry," and I had the feeling my parents would not have cared if I had slapped Charlie.

We finished the dishes and in all innocence I promised Mama I wouldn't cry anymore over such little things. She gave me a thoughtful look and said, "Your tears had nothing to do with it. Why don't we walk to the creek and have a talk?"

Mama gathered up her skirts and we sat on the bank, the water running smooth and clear. Here and there deep pools were still and dark, while other parts were shallow and gurgling as water fell over the gray, smooth rocks. The sound of crickets mingled with an occasional plop of a frog jumping from the sandy bank into the water. With twilight closing in, Mama talked as I listened. I realized on that evening in September 1923, I was beginning to grow up.

Picnic at the Place

There is a warm place in my heart for twenty-three acres of wooded peace one mile south of Nashville, Ohio that belonged to my Grandpa John Van Buren Fisher for many, many years. Among those acres was a small coal mine with a track of some sort and my Papa and Grandpa, wearing hard hats with tiny oil lamps, would push a cart into the mine. Dad and Grandpa worked hard to mine enough coal in one summer to heat both our houses all winter.

Nestled in the trees near the entrance to the mine was a small shed containing a wooden table, two chairs, and pegs where the men would hang their coal-dust covered overalls. The way the trees snuggled the shed gave it a charming coziness. My Mama called those acres "The Place." She would find solace there away from the routine of home.

One fine summer's day, my Mama thought it might be nice to walk a few miles to the Place and surprise our Papa with a picnic lunch. He had not enjoyed working at the Place so much since his Father had died three years earlier. John decided to pull our little red wagon to the back porch and in it Mama placed a round loaf of bread, a jar of apple butter, hard-boiled eggs, cold sliced beef, peach pie, and a jug of lemonade. John and I pulled the wagon up the hill from home and down the dusty road that led to the Place. Small puffs of dust rose up from between the toes of our bare feet as we walked along. Mama told us about the years of World War I when Papa and his brothers had planted enough corn and potatoes to feed their three families and took off enough coal to keep the houses warm during the gusty winter Ohio winds.

During our walk she also reminded us the Place had been in the family during the Civil War when Papa's own Grandma Fisher and Grandma DeWitt watched their sons walk away from their front door to join the Union Army. Likely, the Place gave forth its bounty to sustain those families too, for sustenance was needed to assuage the grief of the Fisher family when three of five sons gave their lives. Patriotic parades in Nashville would thereafter pass Katherine Fisher's home with shades tightly drawn.

As we walked we paused before a large house built by a County Commissioner. We had passed by many times before but for some reason Mama wanted to point out its presence. I noticed then that she needed a spell to stop and look out at the fields. When Mama had a faraway look like that, with big tears in her eyes, I knew she was missing my little sister Amy who had died the previous year. Amy was the baby and four years younger than my siblings and I. No baby to carry on a hip that year. She then turned to us with damp cheeks and announced, "We'd best get to where we're going or all this good food will go to waste." We agreed and continued on.

Our first stop was Grandma's brother, Uncle Gil DeWitt's place. On the porch stood our Great Aunt Laurie, as always in her bare feet, toothless, and smoking her corn cob pipe. Despite our living a rural life, we never got over how eccentric Aunt Laurie seemed and were always a bit taken aback by her grin and her pipe. She gave us all cool water from her well and then joined us on our sojourn to the Place.

Once off the road, we struggled with our wagon while Francie and Helen ran alongside. Forging our own path through the woods, we at last came to the clearing to surprise our delighted Papa. How blue his eyes looked surrounded by a face smudged with coal dust. We each received a big grimy hug in turn, and then Papa took one look at Mama's face and walked her inside the little shed. We all knew she started crying again but thought it would be polite not to notice. Aunt Laurie helped us get settled, singing a song and laughing. The birds sang, bees buzzed, and the sunshine filtered through the trees. We set up our lunch on a fallen log beside a big stone.

We had many picnics at the Place and often relatives joined us. Uncle Wes and Aunt Bertha always brought candy. Uncle Will and Aunt Mat brought oranges that had been shipped all the way from Florida. Their daughter Edna, eighteen, in love and with not much patience for children, would wander away by herself, into the "wilderness" with my father's much-used whistle around her neck on a piece of twine meant to be blown if she became lost. We wondered if our Civil War soldier great uncles were there too, ghosts in the shadows, watching from behind the trees.

We played Hide and Seek and my little sister Helen cried because she was lost behind a tree that was so big she didn't know what direction to turn when she came out from behind it. Soon Mama and Papa joined us—our tall, slender Mama with her long, soft brown braids wrapped around her head as if forming a kind of crown. She was smiling now and I assumed with the innocence of a child, that all memories of loss were forgotten and she would be happy again.

John's First Bike

My home was at the foot of a steep hill and our large yard was fronted by several fields, one of which was used by the neighborhood for a baseball diamond. Now autumn, the field had been mowed several times and was dry and slippery.

Above the fields was the dirt footpath heading to town, worn smooth and grassless by the comings and goings of folks on the edge of town. My ten-year-old brother was learning to ride a bicycle outgrown by our cousin Edna, and we decided to take it past the ball field and up the hill to the path. Once there, I trotted along by his side as he wobbled along on the bike.

A voice from behind us leered "Only sissies ride a girl's bicycle. You are nothing but a great big sissy." John immediately stopped the bike, pushed me aside, strode back to the seventh-grade tease and gave him a wallop which sent him rolling down the field.

Down and down he rolled, tumbling toward the baseball diamond. My eight-year-old heart skipped with delight as I called to my brother, already riding away from me on the bike, "John! Hey John! He landed on first base!" I hollered. John's voice, laughing, came floating back to me, "Yeah, but he couldn't have done it without my help!"

A Tribute to Mama

God could not be everywhere, so he made mothers. –
Jewish Proverb

When the wind blew cold before the first snowfall, my mama knew she would be rearing her family for several months without a husband. My father was in the plastering trade and in those days all building ceased with the approach of cold weather. Papa went to Lakeland, Florida, where there was plenty of work.

I had no idea this bothered my mama. Then came that winter night I remember so vividly. We were in bed; sound asleep between blankets warmed with wrapped hot bricks when I was awakened by a loud noise on the wooden stoop that held the water pump. My brother was shaking me, "Sis, do you hear that? Shouldn't we waken Mom?" "You waken her," I replied, "I'm too scared to get out of bed."

Mama, 39 years old, came over in her flannel nightgown, her hair in two long braids down her back, grabbed a dust mop from a corner, opened the window a bit, pushed out a few inches of the handle and said, "Get off my property or I'll shoot."

The reply came quickly, "Effie, I'm your neighbor—my horse got out and I'm trying to find him. He was on this stoop. I see his hoof prints in the snow."

Mama, who never said an unkind word to anyone, replied, "Mend your fences and fix your barn door and you won't have to hunt your horse in the middle of the night scaring people half to death." She slammed the window.

My brother said, "Gee, you were brave Mom," but I saw her frightened look as she put the mop back in place. She told us to go to sleep. Soon, everything was quiet. I stayed awake. I was so proud of my mama but I hadn't told her so and she always complimented us when a deed was well done.

I went to the small, bare landing at the head of the stairs just outside her room. The floor was cold as ice. The oil lamp, with its wick turned low, made everything look spooky.

Then I heard Mama crying real soft-like and she was saying, "Oh my dear, you must find work at home next winter. I'm so lonely—so lonely." I was puzzled. Mama lonely? With four children around? I decided she wouldn't want me to know she was crying. Just as I was crawling back in bed I remembered the day I was late for school and had to walk the whole way by myself. I was so lonesome for someone to walk beside me. If that was the feeling Mama had, she needed someone too.

I went to her room, snuggled down in her bed—neither of us said a word. I put my small arms around her and nestled my head on her shoulder. Soon my tired, brave mama was asleep. I had such a nice feeling of contentment and pride. I was only 10, but I had done the right thing.

Papa Buys a Car

The manager of the Ford Agency in Lakeland, Florida, looked at his customer in disbelief. "Let me get this right," said the manager to my papa. "You want to buy a car and be taught how to drive it by noon because you have to get to Nashville, Ohio?"

"That's it," my papa confirmed, standing his ground. The manager turned the deal over to a salesman, who stayed with Papa all afternoon. "You oughta have more experience, at least with the reverse," he said to Papa, both of them sweating in the sun.

"I won't park where I need to back up," Papa reassured him. He left late in the afternoon and five days later, we gathered around to hear his story.

He spent his first night at a tourist home because he learned the owners of tourist homes would pack a lunch and fill his Mason jar with water. This was done at each place. Who needed a train? However, the second night was noisy; there was a baby and a two-year old. When Papa wanted breakfast, the baby wanted her bottle, so he fried his own eggs. The day was beastly hot and he was nearly out of gas when he spotted a pump by the curb. "Gosh, it was hot! When I had to stop for a train, I sure wished I was a passenger."

Papa said, "I saw a huge tree in a side yard and a woman on the porch in a rocker, fanning herself. I stopped and told her my story, my need for sleep and could I take a nap in the shade of that big tree. She brought me a pillow and water and I told her not to waken me. At six o'clock I felt a tap on my shoulder and a man said, 'Supper's ready—come and eat with us.' When he learned I liked euchre, he said if I would play a few games, I could stay the night. The next morning his wife, after breakfast, put chipped ice in my Mason jar. I shall never forget those people. We had lots of laughs and I gave him my winnings and more."

That night Papa was too tired to hear our stories so Mama told us we could play outdoors until dark. Finally Mama called us in. Why was Papa too tired to hear our stories, but listened to Mama's all the time? It just didn't make sense to me.

Mama's Haircut

It was summer back in the mid-twenties and the day was warm and the sun was bright. Mama had washed her hair so she took a kitchen chair out by a flowerbed and began reading the Ladies Home Journal while the sun dried her long, wet hair. Before long, she plucked a marigold to use as marker for a special page.

Suddenly, Mama was all action. She rolled her hair up loosely, stuck in a few pins, picked up her magazine and said to my older brother, "John, you are the boss while I make a short trip up town." ("uptown" meant walking the equivalent of three to four blocks up the hill to Main Street.) It wasn't really up the hill but it was due north so maybe that's where we got "up"). Mama took the short cut, crossing the yard, disappearing into a small meadow of tall grasses, past Mrs. Crow's house, across a narrow alley and up a small bank that ended at Main Street.

John and I played ball to the cheering of sisters Francie and little Helen. Later, a woman who looked like Mama walked into the yard… but she wasn't Mama…or was she? She came closer and stopped. "Well, do you like it?" she asked. We were shocked…Mama's hair was cut to just below her ears. John kept staring, I cried, little Helen yelled, "You are not Mama!" and Francie shrieked, "I don't like you anymore!" Just then, Papa came home from work and after one glance at this somber tableau, he knew he had better say the right things. "Well, Effie, what did old Dan the barber say when you came in for a haircut?" No answer. "I must say, you look ten years younger." Mama beamed.

After a rather silent supper, I opened the magazine to the page marked by a wilted marigold and I read to the family…"Bobbed hair is the trend for tomorrow…quit wasting your time washing and drying your long tresses. Begin the future with short hair." Papa said, "Effie, that really took nerve." How scandalous Mama had been—to go into a men's barbershop! We all laughed as he tousled her short, fluffy hair.

Sleepwalkers

My father had severe back pain, something we called "lumbago" in those days. When the pain became unbearable, Uncle Will would drive down from Akron and take him to his cabin in Michigan, which was near a treatment center.

One Spring, in the early twenties, my Grandma went along. Uncle Will was like a son to her because his Mama (Grandma's sister Susannah) had died when she was only forty-two, therefore my Grandma helped to raise him. Grandma took this trip as a sign that she would have an opportunity to be with her two boys. Returning home, we all sat down to supper with Uncle Will as our guest. Papa ate some and then announced he had a story to us. He looked at Uncle Will and asked, "Do you mind, Will?" "Go ahead," he said, as he finished his piece of pie.

Papa began, "As soon as it became dark, we all went to bed because there was nothing to do and I was always tired after a treatment. About midnight, Will heard the outside door open and close so he got up and went to check it out and by golly, he saw Grandma walking towards the water. He followed her and as he got closer, he saw she was fast asleep. Now Uncle Will had heard that you never waken a sleepwalker, but when he saw her walk into the lake, he decided to grab her. However, when Grandma felt the cold water, she quickly turned around, started back toward the cabin, opened the door, and with Will right behind her, closed it, went back to bed, and pulled up the covers.

At breakfast, Will said, with a smile, "Well Aunt Fanny, you sure made an attractive ghost last night when you walked to the lake with all that long white hair blowing with the breeze." Your Grandma, with nary a smile said, 'What in the world are you talking about?' All the way back to Ohio Grandma never said a word and when she reached her home she got out of the car and said, 'Will, I never knew you to lie. I think you had better stay with Bert, Effie, and the children tonight.' Uncle Will came home with Papa and spent the night. We couldn't help wondering if Grandma was afraid to go to sleep that night.

That same year, right after Christmas, Papa left for Florida to plaster houses, and Mama said I could have my friend Jennie for a sleepover. What fun! Mama lightly greased the top of the big old cool stove and thinly sliced potatoes over it. When they became golden, she salted them and we had our first ever potato chips. We slept in the *Posy Room* just off the dining room (which became the kitchen in the winter), so named because of the flower-covered wallpaper.

During the night, I reached over across the covers and couldn't find Jennie! I ran upstairs and wakened Mama and John and we searched every room in the house two times over. Mama told us, in a trembling voice, to get quickly into our warm clothes because Jennie must be a sleepwalker and went outdoors.

We walked outside into a blizzard, a howling wind, and a snow covered porch. John grabbed a post and yelled, "Hold hands!" We searched the yard and Mama stumbled over a bucket that belonged at the water pump. We rounded the house, searched the small black barn with Mollie and

Duke in their stalls, and then the outhouse. We noticed a large drift by the coal shed. We ran our hands through the middle, "Jennnnnie, Jennnnnie," but the wind whistled back, "Not here, not here." Ten year old John decided he would sound like Papa, "I am going to saddle up Mollie and go to the sheriff's home." We went back in the house to get dry gloves and heard a moan coming from the laundry room. We ran there with tears on our cheeks and snow from our galoshes dripping to the floor. There was Jennie, all tangled up in the corner among the clothes line. She had been in there all the time and we didn't notice her standing among all the damp clothes. Mama soon had her in a fresh dry nightie and this time placed her next to the wall in the living room where she couldn't easily get out. Soon all was quiet but just to be on the safe side, I tiptoed into the living room couch, picked up all the cushions and made an extra wall between us and the doorway. It was only then that I slept. Jennie never spent the night again after that.

Reunions at Aunt Della's

There was always a baseball game and uncles always stood by to cheer. My brother was at bat when he noticed a small pouting cousin. "If you stay there, you'll get hit." He didn't budge. John, in the exasperated voice of a 13 year old, yelled, "Will the father of this child remove him from the diamond?" The kid howled, "I wanna play!" Uncle spanked, and we girls, sitting on a grassy knoll, screeched, "Play ball!"

Aunt Della, who was childless, always lost a few flowers when she had the reunion. I'll tell you how. Her sloping lawn was perfect for rolling. One time, eight year old Cy gathered up speed and rolled right over another participant, whose needless screams caused Cy to lose direction and he rolled into a narrow trellis on the corner porch. Crash! For a while all we could see was a mass of leaves, white blossoms of "Star of Bethlehem," and sections of white wood.

Another time, Cy, now twelve, kissed a ten-year-old cousin in front of the golden-glow bush, which was a mass of double, yellow flowers, and she pushed him so hard he fell into the middle of it, thus destroying its beauty for that year. Two more incidents of other years are why I remember Aunt Della's reunions more than the others.

It was like this: a sister, learning the cat was in the hay mow having kittens, quickly climbed the ladder to watch. The boys, full of mischief, removed the ladder. Hearing screams, I went for Uncle Carl. The boys ran helter-skelter and the confused dog pawed his way through a bed of orange and yellow nasturtiums. And one more—Cy, poor kid, when trying to reach a ball that had landed in Aunt Della's short flower bed which went from the kitchen toward the clothesline, lost his balance and fell lengthwise into the flowers.

So, where were all of the parents when all this was going on? The mothers were gathered around a table, talking with honeyed voices; the fathers formed a group of their own to worry about crops, get excited about politics, or reminisce sadly about those who had passed on. The day ended at milking time. How relieved Aunt Della must have been.

Why Did Grandpa Marry Grandma?

I was just a child when I began to wonder why Grandpa married Grandma. That was an odd thing to consider at such a tender age, but I was always trying to figure things out. They had such different dispositions. Grandpa was jolly and full of smiles and Grandma always seemed rather grim.

I passed their house going to and from school and when I was going home Grandpa, more often than not, would be sitting in his rocker on the porch that faced Main Street. I would run and climb on his lap, throw my arms around his neck and snuggle into his warm embrace. He always called me by my middle name, Kathryn, and I never asked why. "Surely," I thought, "there must have been a Kathryn somewhere in his past."

Our magic spell was often broken by Grandma asking me to go to the corner grocery or bring a jar of preserved vegetables or jam up from the cellar. I finally decided Grandma had a jealous streak running though her. She was jealous because I always went to Grandpa. Aunt Alda once told me jealousy was a green-eyed monster, but Grandma was certainly not that! It was a difficult thing for me to understand.

My grandparents seemed to get along, but they sure did approach matters differently. Take for instance, the well in the side-yard. Grandma gathered us four children together and said, in a very stern voice, "Don't you ever go near the well. You could fall in and drown." But Grandpa, he took us to that well, showed us the bucket, unwound the rope and let the bucket go down and be filled with cool, delicious water. We heard a faint splash and back up it came as he wound the rope round and round and back in place. Then, he held us up over the stone wall of the well, and one at a time we peered down into the cool, damp, bottomless depth, dark and frightening, eerie and profound. "Now," he said, "you have seen it and don't ever come over here again because I don't want to lose you."

Then there was the matter of the garden. No one had bigger or better vegetables. We loved seeing them piled in a basket, (our enthusiasm waned however when we were instructed to pick off the ugly potato bugs and drop them into a little pail of hot water). Grandpa took great pride in his garden and he loved flowers and sunset and fields and blooming weeds. He had even planted flowering bushes, the old-fashioned sweet scented mock-orange, to screen the outhouse. Grandma, however, seemed only to be outside and in the garden when she needed something to cook for supper. She didn't even pause to enjoy the aroma or colors of the peppers or tomatoes like Grandpa did, she just walked out, picked them, and hurried back inside to cook.

It seemed Grandma was always cleaning, cooking, and baking. That was fine with me because the cookie jar was never empty when I stopped by after school. I do remember that because they lived right on Main

Street, there was a lot of dust coming in through the windows before they paved that road. That seemed to always bother Grandma.

Grandma just never seemed to have the time for us. Grandpa was the one who did. As I was the eldest girl and stopped by their home after school most frequently, I had the opportunity to spend a little more time with Grandma than my siblings. Grandma had always been good to my Mama, but when we were alone, she would find fault with her. She often remarked, "your Mama would be a better housekeeper if she didn't take all those walks with you children." Those comments hurt, and feelings of dislike would well up in me. I never told Mama what she said, because I thought it would bother her, but I never forgot the things my Grandma said.

I did discuss this with my Grandpa one day. It was on that occasion he told me they once had a daughter—a beautiful daughter, Estella, who at school one day had a chair pulled out from her by a teasing boy and her back was broken. She never walked again, becoming, in those days, what one called an "invalid." Grandpa told me that he thought Grandma was jealous because our Mama had three girls and that Estella's death had "just changed her." "But Grandpa," I said, "she was your daughter too." He gave a long sigh that faded away.

Joy of Spring

"Spring is God's way of saying, 'One more time!'" — Robert Orben

It was spring and I felt bubbles of happiness inside. I wanted to do flip-flops on the lawn, skip rope, catch a ball – everything I couldn't do all winter. Grandma, taking down the wash, had her mouth full of clothespins. "Where's Grandpa?" I yelled. She pointed to the barn.

I skipped down the narrow walk that led to the "necessity" as my Mama always called it, crossed the dirt alley and skipped lightly to the rear of the barn where I found my Grandpa Fisher. "My gosh, Kathryn, (he always called me by my middle name and I never thought to ask why) it's too nippy to have your coat open. Come here and feel the warmth of my arm."

"Look at the sweep of those fields," he said, "and the rims of the hills; now and then I feel the sky is trying to touch them. None of it is mine but I've admired this view for so long – if anything happened to it —well, I would probably drop dead."

We walked slowly to the house. "You know child, the vegetable garden looks too big to plant this year – I even dread clearing it in the fall." I bounced ahead and looked up at him with loving eyes, "Do you feel sick, Grandpa?" He gave a tired smile, "No my dear, just old." I shivered, buttoned my coat and grasped his hand and felt, in a childlike way, that we left spring behind the barn.

Spring and Fall, Gardens and Fathers

Grandpa planted his garden but that fall he was coming from the cellar and fell on his face in the spot that had been green with the spring. Just like that, he was gone. Leaning against the unpainted barn, where he always stood, I cried my heart out. I wished Grandpa could have died in the spring so that his dear white head could have fallen on a pillow of lettuce leaves. An autumn chill hovered. I touched my shoulder, hoping to feel Grandpa's rugged hand. An early sunset bathed "his" fields in gold.

The funeral was held at his home. I did not want to go and see Grandpa like that, but Grandma insisted. She had chairs in the living room for the relatives and Grandpa's casket, flanked by fancy oil lamps on pedestals at each end, stood in the corner of the dining room. I was upset because it wasn't in the front room where the sun came streaming through the lace curtains and his favorite friend's house was right across the street. I thought Grandpa would have liked that.

The next day after school, I didn't walk past Grandpa's but instead took an alley below Main Street, then a foot path and finally down the grassy hill to home. Mama met me at the door and with a kind look said, "Grandma is very lonely." The next day I stopped there after school, gave Grandma my best hug and sat down in Grandpa's rocker. With each bite of my sugar cookie I tried to figure out why Grandpa had died, and there across the street was his best friend who was not only alive, but was working away in his garden to boot. I would have to talk with Mama about that.

Remembering Bedtime Rituals

After Grandpa died, Grandma wanted me to spend my nights with her. But I didn't want to and in order for you to understand why, I shall tell you about my evenings at home, which were special and lots of fun.

After supper, Mama had a clever way of getting us to help. She would get out the big dish pan, fill it with hot water from the stove reservoir, another pan for rinsing, and then she would sing, "John, bring me some plates to wash; Helen, gather the knives, forks and spoons; Francie, bring the glasses as we sing a merry tune." I tried to dry as fast as my Mama washed.

Now it was time for our game of *Parcheesi*. We were a cozy little group at one end of the kitchen table. There was so much laughter that if Papa had been there (he worked during the week in Canton; too far away to drive back for just the night) he would call out, "Quiet down out there." Then, it was cookies and milk, prayers and bed, mom lulling us to sleep with her piano music.

Then Grandpa died and every evening after supper I walked up the hill and down Main Street to Grandma's, who was sitting in her rocker and crying. She would later read the Bible out loud. "Are you listening?" she would ask and I would say "yes," but I was really thinking about Parcheesi.

One night I cried as I was leaving and Mom told my brother John he would have to go instead. He didn't mind because he liked Grandma's high bed. But I heard Mama say to Papa "something has to be done about your Mother—this is not fair to the children." That same evening something happened that solved her problem.

I was finishing my glass of milk when John, still in his nightclothes, burst into my room crying and saying, "Grandma is dead and it's all my fault!" Father said, "Let's not waste time – you can tell me about it on the way." My disturbed Mama nodded that I could go, too. John, between sobs, began telling his story and this is how I remember it in his words.

"I had gone to bed and woke up because my room was like daylight and from bed I could see a big, round, yellow moon shining right at me—it was like magic. I opened the window and leaned out so I could see everything and the big branch of the apple tree looked so close I was sure that by leaning out a little more, I could touch it and that's when I hit the ground.

I ran around the house and pounded on the front door. Grandma finally opened it and when she saw me she said, "Merciful heavens" and fell flat on the floor. I couldn't waken her so I knew she was dead."

Father put his arm around John and said, "Son, I think your grandma fainted—after all, you were supposed to be in bed." When we reached her porch the door was still open and Grandma was trying to get up. Although she was a small woman, John and I still had to help her get on her feet.

John said he would stay, but Grandma, to our surprise, stood up real straight, threw back her shoulders, held her head high and told John he could tell her about it tomorrow. "Right now, I want you to go home. Grandpa is dead and I must learn to stay alone, beginning tonight."

I thought it so strange…it was as though she just now realized Grandpa had died and it happened weeks before, but stranger than that was the fact that John, unknowingly, solved Mama's problem. Or, should I say, John and the moon. A few years later, Grandma met an old school beau, married him and went to live in his house in Danville. The year was 1923.

Little White Lies

Munching on graham crackers, I tramped through the dry leaves of fall trying to see how much noise I could make. Still hungry, it seemed like a good idea to stop at Grandma's and see what she had to eat. Running in the door, I shouted "Hi, graham cracker," and then, realizing the slip of the tongue, I laughed and kept on laughing until I apprehended she was angry and saying I showed no respect for older people. I tried to explain but she kept on talking and said, "No cookies for you today."

I took the long way home to do some thinking. I decided Grandma had never really been young—should I tell Mama about it? No, why bother her. I tried to change my thoughts. There were so many different sizes of leaves on the ground. I thought of winter coming and how the kids would be sled-riding down our hill. Who cared about cookies—it was almost supper time.

Mama was at the kitchen table sorting the last basket of clothes fresh from the clothes line. The kitchen smelled like open air—fresh and clean. I could hear my brother calling to a sister in the field. The cat was meowing at the back door. Mama took one look at me and asked if I wanted to talk about it. My feelings were showing like a petticoat too long for the dress. I moved a chair to where the sun's rays warmed the kitchen, sat down, blurted it all and noticed at the same time how tired Mama looked on wash day.

Mama thought it funny the way words come out all wrong and then with a serious look, explained that some people were born without a sense of humor, could be more fault-finding than others and didn't know how important it was to be understanding of young folks. "We must learn to accept people the way they are because they may never change, but I still keep trying to figure her out."

Just then a sharp voice was heard at the door saying, "Are you talking about me?" Mama replied quite calmly she was telling me about an old school friend. Grandma then asked me for an apology concerning the earlier incident and Mama said, "Once you hear the explanation you will find no apology necessary." She listened, said she was sorry, chatted a bit and left. I knew there would be cookies the next day.

I was proud of the way it was handled but in a mischievous manner, I said, "Mama, you lied to Grandma and you are a Sunday school teacher." She told me it was a little white lie and that was different. "Why hurt your grandmother needlessly—it would make things difficult for a long time. Even your father might not understand."

"How do you know when to tell a white lie?" Mama responded, "Kindness, tact, understanding and a few little white lies all come in the same package. A white lie makes you feel good whereas a black lie makes you feel miserable and will hurt others as well as yourself."

While she was at the stove checking on supper, my father returned from putting in long hours trying to finish the plastering in a new home before cold weather set in. Placing his lunch bucket on the table, he looked at me and asked if I had a good day. In a breezy manner, I replied, "My day was fine—just fine." I felt all aglow—I had not upset my weary parents. I looked at Mama. She nodded her head ever so slightly, winked and smiled.

A Close Call at the Dinner Table

It was Christmas in the mid-1920s and Mama, Papa and we four children were blown into Grandmas' cozy kitchen with a flurry of snow. Grandma, always prompt, had dinner ready, so we went quickly to the chest and hall tree in the corner and discarded boots and damp coats. Our gloves were sodden for during the mile-long walk from home, we made and threw snowballs.

I was always amazed how Grandma's sitting room could be transformed into a dining room, the table for eight (sadly now set for only seven since Grandpa had died) was set with the best of everything. Small, curved, flowered bone dishes at each place, tiny salt and peppers wells scattered here and there. On the white tablecloths were napkins large enough to cover your entire lap with some hanging down a bit on each side. The centerpiece was a beautiful cake with lots of white frosting, sitting on a glass pedestal dish. Pies were on the worktable in the kitchen. Pretty flowered plates (now dispersed through the family) were waiting for food.

Soon all bowls and tureens were filled and taken to the table. We bowed our heads for Grandma's prayer and once she began, she did not know when to stop. Finally, Papa said, "Mother, that's enough praying—the food is getting cold." Just like that, Grandma left a sentence hanging in mid-air and said "Amen" and began passing the scrumptious food.

The meal progressed smoothly, I know my parents were proud of our behavior (nothing spilled) remembering to say "please" and "thank you" (Grandma was soooooo proper) and then it happened! Mama had turned towards Grandma telling her of an incident at the Ladies Aid Society and saw that Grandma was choking. Papa raced to the kitchen, came back with an egg, cracked it on the table, and with Mama holding Grandma's head back, dropped its contents down her throat.

We children were staring at this frightening tableau in disbelief and I was so proud that my parents knew what to do. Grandma quickly recovered and in her prim manner, sat up straight and said, "Thank you Herbert—now let's have our cake and pie."

Once the dishes were done, Papa took all perishables to the cold cellar, put more coal in the stoves, refilled the coal buckets and made sure the pail had water. Then we sat around and listed to Victrola records.

Time to bundle up once more. Grabbing our mittens from atop the black cookstove where they had warmed and dried, we went out the door into the falling snow yelling "Merry Christmas" to the entire neighborhood. Amidst much laughter, Dad threw the first snowball. I, always the serious one, talked to Mama about Grandma. "This Christmas dinner surely was different", I noted. Mama took my hand and replied, "Throughout your life each Christmas will, in some way, be unlike the one before. Each year brings changes, but the true meaning of Christmas never changes." The snow kept falling as my siblings ran ahead.

A Colony of Aunts

Whenever I think of my Mama's older sister Alda, I see her with children. She reared four of her own under difficult conditions and when a daughter died while still a young mother, took those four grandchildren including twin boys. Later, when a granddaughter had marital problems, she took into her arms a great-grandson and many times, his two sisters. All this in a small city apartment. Children were her life. She often found time to visit us and help Mama make our clothes. They would sew for hours, laughing and talking. We loved her dearly.

Aunt Mat was a large imposing woman. She never invited affection but we felt her love as sure as if she'd held her arms wide to receive us. She and Uncle Will visited often, coming in their big shiny car from the city of Akron where she had a live-in maid, to our tiny house in the country. There were always gifts for everyone and each summer some of us stayed with her for a week or more. I was fond of her but never at ease in her presence.

There was a mystery about Aunt Mat because of the big, black, heavy-looking pocketbook she carried all over our house, even keeping it on her arm when helping Mama with the meals. She said she had a hiding place for it on every floor of her home. Mama was as curious about it as we were.

One night, brother John, Aunt Mat and I started home from Grandma's house after dark. John walked in front, swinging the lantern. You could see one minute and the next, you couldn't. Along side the road that went down towards our house was a small ditch, not much different from a rut in the road, but at the foot of a hill it became much deeper. Unknown to us, our Aunt, who was bringing up the rear, was walking along in the ditch. Before long, we heard a scream and that big, black bag landed at my feet. We yelled, "Are you down there Aunt Mat?" We knew she wasn't hurt when she replied, "Of course I'm down here, where is my pocketbook?" Before I helped her out of the ditch, I had to hand over that pocketbook. She placed it back on her arm and it kept banging against me again and again as John and I pushed and pulled to get her out of that ditch.

That night at bedtime, my brother and I decided we had been pretty stupid. We could have left our Aunt in the ditch just long enough for us to see what was in that big black purse. We didn't even think of money—we were sure it was filled with jewels that would glisten and shimmer from the lantern's yellow light, just like a frosted window pane does with a glimmer of sun. The mystery was never solved but over the next few years, that pocketbook would have had to reach the ground to hold everything we decided was in it. I still like to think it was filled with diamonds, rubies, and pearls.

In the days of my youth there always seemed to be an aunt or uncle coming to visit. Some I see so vividly it's like having talked with them last week. Others I barely remember. Aunt Barbara and beautiful hair go together. She has no face in my memories nor do I recall anything she ever said or did. Most are thought of with love, others not so kindly.

Aunt Susan was not a favorite of mine. Tall and slender, prissy and exacting, she was always company when she came to visit—you know what I mean? We told Mama that we knew Aunt Susan didn't like us; children bothered her and we knew it. She and Papa never hit it off too well either, but Mama always defended her saying we couldn't all be alike.

One fine summer day we were to go to her house for lunch, or "dinner" as we called it then. Mama asked a neighbor to drive us the thirty miles in his "tin lizzie." During the previous week she has us practice our best table manners saying each evening, "Now pretend you are in Aunt Susan's beautiful dining room." My brother John teased her and said he was going to spill something on purpose. When we curled up on our old couch at night, Mama reminded us we must be careful of our Aunt's sofa which was covered with velvet. That morning we dressed in our Sunday closes which made us uncomfortable because it wasn't Sunday.

When we arrived, Aunt Susan met us at the back door, took one look at us and said almost immediately, "Since it is such a hot day I thought we would enjoy eating in the basement." She didn't fool us. We knew she didn't want children in her dining room. Down the stairs we went where she had a table set with candles which were surely needed in such a gloomy room. My Mama barely touched her food. When we were finished my aunt asked if we children wouldn't like to take a walk. We trudged along for several blocks and John said, "We're not even going to see the old fuss budget's velvet couch, let alone sit on it."

Upon our return, Mama was waiting for us. "Children", she said, "we are going to start for home. Please say your goodbyes." We also said "thank you" without being reminded. Once we were back in the old Ford she turned to us and said, "You and your father were right about Aunt Susan, and in many ways your manners are better than hers. Now we'll say no more about it."

Mama was not easily offended but this time she felt her loved ones had been insulted and we could tell she was deeply hurt. A hurt like that is penetrating, slow to heal and often not forgotten. Aunt Susan sometimes visited us after that, but we never again visited her.

Valentine's Day

In my class was a boy from a family of ten. He had a mop of curly hair and a nice smile. His clothes were either too small or too large and he always needed a haircut. I had noticed he was often alone. I told my Mama, who thought the fair way to send valentines was to draw names, but then I was afraid Troy would not get a valentine and she replied, "Then give him one." So, I did, but I didn't sign it.

The next morning I dropped my cards in the slot of the box. They were beautifully decorated with white paper lace and red hearts. When the teacher called Troy's name, everyone looked surprised and it was the only valentine he received.

It was my day to stay after school and help the teacher; when I walked out the door Troy was standing there in the cold. "Troy," I said, "you have missed your ride home." "I know," he said, "but I wanted to thank you for my valentine." "But how did you know it was from me?" I replied. "Because," he answered, "you are the only one in the class kind enough to do it," and he ran down the steps.

I started for home in deep thought. How awful to go to school each day and feel no one cared about you. A cold wind clutched at my valentines and I held them tightly. Mr. Thome opened the door of his grocery store and said, "Better hurry my young friend, it is going to snow." I thought of Troy walking alone on a country road with snow clouds hovering and I wanted to cry.

It was snowing hard as I went down the hill to home. Mama held the door open and I blew right in. Of course, I told her about Troy. She told me I had received a nice compliment, but I said I didn't deserve it because I wasn't thoughtful enough to sign my name. "Why didn't you sign your name?" I knew the answer—I didn't want anyone to know. Mama told me to go on being kind and I would feel good about myself again.

I went to bed feeling very unhappy. There was just nothing I could do or say—Troy knew I didn't want others to know—after all, he was a smart boy.

It snowed a lot that night and Mom and John were out making a path up the hill. I wished my father, who was in Florida plastering new houses, were home to help. Finally John, Francie and I got bundled up, galoshes and all, to walk to school. Little Helen was still in bed.

When I entered the school rooms, some of the kids were standing in a group and they motioned to me—I went over. "Who do you think sent Troy the valentine?" I was asked. "I did," I replied, and then turning to the boys, I added, "And I think if you had Troy on your baseball team this spring you would win a lot more games." I was later breathing so fast I felt dizzy and I hurried to my seat. Later, I told Mama I had no idea where all those words came from and she smiled, "They came from your heart."

But do you know what? Troy was asked that spring to be on the team and on February 14th he received lots of valentines and the one from me read, "Your friend, Alathea."

Independence Day

As a child, my favorite holiday, next to Christmas, was Fourth of July. Decorating the front lawn with flags was as festive an occasion as decorating the Christmas tree.

My Mama loved small flags. She even placed them along the footpath going from the back door to the chicken yard, thus making a dirt walkway look very special. She then gave each of us ten flags to place wherever we pleased. My favorite spot was around the golden-glow bush; my two sisters did the porches.

One year my brother, John, age nine, refused to tell us where he put his flags. When we went to feed the horses, we found them in a neat row in front of the stalls of Mollie and Duke. My Mama was a little put out.

John, who loved history, said, "Mom, I think you are forgetting how important horses were during the Civil War. And I bet when Thomas Jefferson drew up the Declaration of Independence his horse was tied outside." I thought it must be great to be so smart and Mama told him he was right and the flags looked real nice there.

Mama was pianist for the Methodist Church and one year she thought it would be great for her piano students to put on a drill for the Fourth of July. She drew the drill procedures on sheets of wrapping paper and then gave each pupil coming for a music lesson a note, in her bold handwriting, stating practice dates and time. She had to think ahead because the only phone in town was at the telephone office.

Practice began in June at the church. We got so tired of going that Mama devised different ways to get there which lent a great deal of excitement to the walk. One time we walked through a field that took us by the lock-up, a small one-room building for people in trouble with the law. It had bars across two small windows and we always pretended someone was in there and we would run real fast to get by. We named everything and this was called the lock-up trail. Another time we walked through the rows of vegetables in the garden, each one a different row, and this brought us to the back door of the church so it became the back-door road. Once, we cut through alleys that reached Main Street and ended at the front door—so we called that the alley route. Going to practice for the drill became great fun.

The church was packed on the sunny, hot afternoon of the Fourth of July. Mama was thrilled when she saw the three commissioners outside looking in the open window at the one end of the so-called stage. Later, I heard her tell Papa, "Even the commissioners came to see the drill," and Papa mumbled something and arched his eyebrows. The drill began with each of us carrying a little flag which we used in different motions and no one got out of step as we sang "Yankee Doodle Dandy" loud and clear to wild applause.

That night we walked up town to a big tent in an empty lot, circling our sparklers and sitting with grandpa and grandma, who brought some fudge for us to eat while the program was going on. I don't remember any fireworks.

Halloween Parade

It is that time of year when you see sun filtering through the foliage an hour or more before it high-lights the crown canopy. Apples, not gathered from the ground, exude an unpleasant odor, cut-outs of black cats, witches and ghosts appear on windows and doors and smiling pumpkin faces are seen on porches and fence posts.

Effie Fisher, mother of four, was frustrated and downcast during the time of goblins. She was frustrated because she could not talk her children into participating in the Halloween Parade, even though she was a fine seamstress and had scads of ideas for costumes. She was also downcast because her husband went south where he could find work during winter months plastering new houses.

Much to the children's surprise, their tall, slender, beautiful mother was not going to the parade. "You go," she said, come straight home and we'll eat popcorn. You won't need a flashlight—there's a full moon."

The parade started on time and just when everyone thought it was over, down the street came a lone person, white hair hanging to her hips, a white face, and a full-skirted innovative costume of quilt blocks with a bodice of the deepest color, (which was purple) with raglan sleeves. After walking regally, she would act like a clown, skipping to each side, her hair blowing across her face, and chanting, "You don't know me—or who I be," and then she would laugh like—well, like a witch would laugh.

At the judge's stand, she bowed and said, "Look me over, while I am here—for very soon, I shall disappear." As she moved towards the amazed group of other participants she cried, "WhooOOOOOoooooooo" in a crescendo that slowly ended with a deep, scary, guttural groan.

The judges asked all those in costume to pass the reviewing stand; "Tonight we have a new category—a first prize for an outstanding act goes to the woman with the long, white hair. Come forward, please." No one appeared.

Effie's children ran home, eager to tell her what she had missed. "Mom," they yelled and from the living room came the reply; "WhoooOOOOOooooo." She was soon engulfed by loving arms and hearing the compliments that were like piano music to her ears.

The popcorn was ready and as they ate, admiring children were told how their mother had practiced her walk, her tone of voice and did her sewing while they were in school. Then, with papers spread on the floor, each child took a turn at brushing the flour from her chestnut-brown hair.

Finally, all was quiet. Effie sprawled across her bed. My, but parades were exhausting. Her hair, usually wound in three braids around her head, sifted over the bed, and part of her costume, concocted from her mother's quilt patches, cascaded over the side and made a colorful splash on the floor; Effie knew she was going to fall asleep. She was so tired, but so pleased with herself—imagine, all of main street for a stage.

She was never in another parade, but in the early twenties she organized a drama group of people with latent talents and hidden desires and directed three plays which she took to neighboring schools. She also composed drills and assembled programs for patriotic holidays, besides giving piano lessons. Her potential had been released on a crisp, fall evening in a small town Halloween Parade.

Mama's Fifth Christmas. A Story Told

Christmas often found Mama at her "desk" at the end of our kitchen table where she did most of her busy work. This time of year often found her making our home made Christmas cards surrounded by red and green painted borders that she would create after supper dishes were done. One Christmas Mama came across a story she had written. It was called, "My Fifth Christmas" by Effie Brown. Following is my mother's story."

"The year was 1886 and I was five years old. I had an older sister, Alda, and three older brothers, Wesley, Walter, and Carl. So you see, I was the baby and I took advantage of that. At least, that's what Alda said.

Every night since my fourth Christmas I prayed for a doll with straight hair that I could curl. When Ma had us kneel to say our prayers, I would always add, "Please see to it that I get a doll with straight hair for Christmas." My brothers got tired of hearing this and Wes said that God heard me the first time and wrote it down in a big black book with a large clasp of solid gold. After that, I made my request beneath the covers.

In those years we had a large tree in the church and it was called the family tree because everyone brought their decorations from home. Our parents placed their children's gifts beneath the tree to be given the Sunday before Christmas.

Finally the day arrived and the smell of breakfast, especially ma's hot rolls, wafting up to our rooms, made us rush for the stairs. Because Ma was afraid we might spill something on our good clothes, we were allowed, on Sundays, to eat breakfast in our nightclothes and bedsocks. What a sight we must have been—Alda and I in our long nighties and nightcaps and our brothers in their long, white flannel nightshirts that reached just below their knees. Ours had pretty collars and theirs just three or four buttons. Pa and Ma were in their Sunday best.

Alda and I went to the parlor to get dressed; then our brothers—the upstairs was too cold. As Alda and I pulled up our stockings, she asked, "Will you act up if you don't get your doll?" I told her I was so sure I'd get my doll that I was taking a muffler to keep her warm.

Pa had decorated the surrey with branches of pine and had placed bells on the horses that jingled as we went down the long lane and on to church where we left the warm robes and walked the snow-shoveled path into the warmth of the church.

After the sermon, Mrs. Jones ascended the platform wearing a beautiful white dress with red bows and Ma, in her pretty dark print, said to Pa, "My, my, my," whatever that meant. Mrs. Jones began calling names and when she said, "Effie Brown," I ran up the aisle only to be handed a small, flat package, definitely not a doll. I hurried back to our pew, tears streaming down my face and trying to control my sobs. I tossed the package onto Ma's lap. She noted, "It's a beautiful red silk sampler." I said, "I hate it," and slumped down in my seat. Ma whispered, "It's from your teacher and she is right behind you." And then she wiped my eyes and said softly, "You still get a gift from Pa and me."

My name was called again and I refused to get up until Alda gave me a shove. I was so ashamed and I hung my head. Mrs. Jones said, "I think this is what you wanted." I unwrapped it right then and there and everyone clapped when I hugged Amy Hilda, a name I chose a year ago.

I later told my teacher I really loved her sampler and in a kind voice she whispered, "Mrs. Jones should have given you the doll first."

Back home I hugged my parents again and Pa, pulling me up on his lap said, "Remember child, you won't always get what you want, so learn to control your emotions; thank God for remembering."

I played with Amy Hilda until I was almost thirteen and one day, Ma, who believed once you were through with something you gave it to someone who needed it, suggested I should give it to some little girl who wanted a doll, and, although it hurt, that is exactly what I did. The End."

I leaned back in my chair. I had been totally unaware that my dear baby sister, Amy Hilda, who had died at age two, had been named after beloved doll.

Blue Satin Mules

I didn't realize it at the time but Christmas, for me in my 11th year, started in the fragrant spring, when, walking down Main Street to keep dental appointments, we passed a shoe store. In the window was a pair of mules (bedroom slippers—these had high heels, minus straps to fit around the heels of the feet).

They were of satin in morning-glory blue with a mound of feathers in a deeper shade which reminded me of our neighbor's delphinium. I had never seen anything so beautiful. I longed to touch them and couldn't hide my yearning from Mama who, with an understanding heart, went in to ask the price. "We'll talk about it on the way home," she said.

Later, we three girls sat in the back seat eating raisins (always a promised treat after the dentist) and Mama turned around and said it was impossible to buy me anything so expensive (I've forgotten the cost) that I wouldn't even wear—but, "If you earn the money, you may buy them."

I became quite excited. My brother, John, said only rich people had things like that and if we were rich he sure wouldn't be driving this old flivver. Mama compared it to wanting a doll so fragile you couldn't play with it.

The next morning I went to the post office and scrawled my name on the "berry pickers wanted" list and work soon started. Strawberries didn't bring in much because too many people signed up. Even though we kept eating them, boxes filled up quickly. At week's end I dropped my pay, one coin at a time, into a glass jar, savoring the clinking sounds.

The boxes for red raspberries and blueberries seemed bottomless, but blackberry season was the most difficult. In spite of Mama's black, cotton stockings, my arms were scratched. Only two of us worked the bushes and I was cross and tired.

I also picked ground cherries which tasted like medicine, helped a neighbor pick peas, beans and get corn ready for drying, and was paid for gathering eggs by an enthusiastic aunt. I helped Grandpa shell hickory nuts and hung up and took down the wash for Mama's ailing friend, who seemed pretty peppy to me.

Each Saturday night we counted the money as we ate ice cream. By "school bell" time, there wasn't enough. It then became a family project. John helped unload coal and dropped his change in the jar. Papa put in some more and Mama gave the money from one pupil's piano lesson (thirty-five cents for an hour) and we made it.

On a wintery-dark day we went for the slippers. The clerk said, "It's been a long time but I knew you would be back after paying fifty cents down." I looked at Mama in amazement – what faith she had in me.

I placed the slippers on a chair by my bed and each night blew softly on the feathers (which seemed to dance to concealed music) and then snuggled under the covers, no longer a flannel-clad, pig-tailed child, but a fairy princess.

Christmas Day Mama made an oval nest of pine clippings for the dining table and in it placed the beautiful slippers, toe to toe. Everyone admired the centerpiece and on that day I became 12 years old.

Many years later when our parents joined other loved ones we cleared out the old home. Reaching into dark recesses of wardrobes I hoped, with a wistfulness, to find an old shoe box containing a pair of blue satin slippers with feathers, no doubt, too flattened to dance, but it was not to be. It's just as well, I sighed. It's just as well.

1

2

3

See photo list on page 127

4

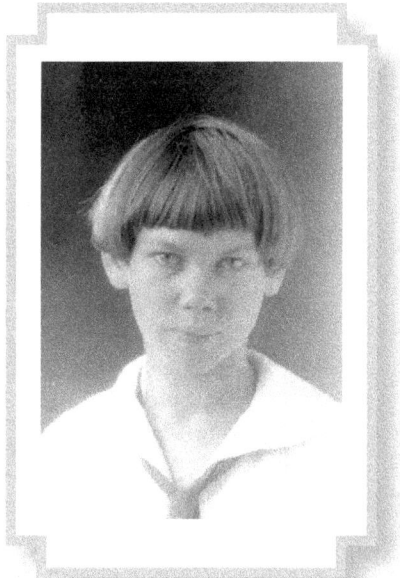

5

6

7

8

9

10

11

12

13

14

15

16

17

18

19

20

21

22

23

24

25

A Tree for Mama

It was one of those clear, bitter cold days in November. I wondered how it was possible for the black, barren trees to produce green leafage each spring. Some of the dark branches reached out independently, boldly defying the elements; others were intertwined and some clustered in groups like relatives at a family reunion.

A friend had promised Mama a Christmas tree but it was up to us to cut it and get it home. Our father had already gone to Florida for winter work and Mama, because of snow filled clouds, was skeptical about my brother and me going a mile into the country without an adult. We finally won her over.

The silence was so profound that even though John was always ahead of me, I could hear every twig snap and the rustle of leaves. I ran to catch up. "Hey John," I yelled, "We are the only ones out here in the country. Who will save us if the ice isn't frozen solid on the creek?" He replied we weren't likely to drown in a creek where we went wading each summer.

We came to the edge of the field where sifted snow lay as lightly on the ground as the sugar sprinkled on Grandma's cookies still warm from the oven. John decided the dry corn stubbles would ruin the tree as we dragged it home. "Let's go along the edge of the field and break a path through the weeds," he said. Walking side by side we managed to tramp down enough sick-looking golden rod to make a trail.

We safely crossed the frozen creek and entered the hilly pine grove. On the other side were the younger trees. We lingered long enough to absorb some of the warmth and I decided that some day I was going to have a pine woods just big enough to feel lost in and yet know that I wasn't.

It took awhile to find a tree big enough. Then we saw it—all alone and easy to chop down. We wound cord around the branches as far as we could reach and when it fell to the ground, we finished the job. "This is a nice size," said John, as he expertly tied roped around the base with big loops at the end so it would be easy to pull.

Half-way across the field a cold wind started hitting us in the face. It didn't just blow past and across the meadow but circled around like it was lost. By the time we reached the back lane going to the barn I was near tears and John said he had never been so cold and tired in his life.

We decided if Mama saw how miserable we were she wouldn't enjoy the tree, so we got the bright idea of going in the barn and thawing out a bit. I went to blind Mollie's stall, tossed my mittens on a straw pile, buried my cold hands in her mane and laid my face against her neck. Dear old Mollie. John did the same with Duke. The horses whinnied at this unexpected affection and their soothing warmth lessened the painful icy tingle on fingertips and cheeks, but it would take hot cocoa and the kitchen range to really thaw us out.

Feeling better, we opened the door and it was snowing like crazy—not just big soft flakes, but so thick we could hardly see the house. We decided to sing Jingle Bells so Mama would think it had all been lots of fun. As we pulled the tree up on the little porch outside the small square living room, she opened the door immediately and said she has been worried sick and here we were looking as if it had been no trouble at all. She measured it for height and brushed it off here and there.

It wasn't easy getting it into the room because we had to make a turn from the hall. We put the tree in the high crock which was ready in its allotted space between the piano and couch. Mama said we had better tie it to the window pull before we took the cords off the branches, as the crock might not hold it steady.

Finally it was time to free the branches, and we weren't prepared for the results. They flung out in all directions, scratching the window panes, hiding the piano bench and a third of the couch and swishing the sheet music to the floor. Mama was amazed. "Goodness gracious, the whole woods is in this room!" In tired but excited voices we told her it wasn't that big in the pine grove. She laughed and said it probably grew some in that long trip home.

During the holidays our high school cousins came from the city for an afternoon. We put on a little program. First, Christmas carols. Even though we had snipped off some branches near the piano, when Mama was on the bench we couldn't see her and it was like the piano was playing all by itself. Then our cousins did the dance craze known as the Charleston. Their feet flew, the room trembled, the pictures on the piano toppled over, the cat scurried to the kitchen, the popcorn strings shifted positions on the tree and even the smaller lumps of coal in the bucket seemed to move a bit.

That night in our bedroom we tried to dance those intricate steps on the wooden floor in our bare feet, laughing so hard we couldn't seem to stop. Mama looked disturbed and after we said our prayers and crawled in between the blankets she said, "It just doesn't seem right to me – singing those beautiful carols and then your cousins doing that crazy dance. Let's sing one verse of "Silent Night.""

It was all so wonderful. The world was such a happy place – so full of love and kindness and understanding. I had just turned thirteen on Christmas Day and at that tender age and in that era, my home was the world.

The Christmas Coat

There was to be a Christmas party for seventh and eighth grades at the town hall, and I had a new rose-colored dress with ruffles around the throat and a coat "made over" by my Mama. When Aunt Della gave her the coat of black plush with big brown plush buttons and a brown fur collar, she said, "You're so good with needle and thread and I want you to make it smaller for Alathea."

Mama thought the colors too old for a teenager, but knowing I needed a coat, she went to work laying it full length on the dining room table. Now and then I would try it on and I seemed to feel Aunt Della's presence; it wasn't a pleasant emotion since she was not a favorite aunt. Mama said it would be much easier to make something brand new.

Party night arrived and my girlfriend and I joined the group in the cold little hall, at the top of the stairs, where there was a long, round rod with hangers and a shelf below for boots and such. Little puddles of melting snow were forming on the wooden floor.

I received no comments on my coat and was ready to put it on the hanger when I heard gasps of astonishment—there, at the foot of the stairs, stood the "new" girl in school who loved to make a late entrance to show off her "store-bought" clothes. Her coat was a bright Christmas red with a soft, thick, black fur collar on which snowflakes still glistened. She looked beautiful.

My heart fell with one thump to my shoes—it wasn't that I was jealous, because that was wicked, but I felt old, old, old in my black coat. I even imagined my hair was turning gray like Aunt Della's. After the party, I made my way down the long hill that led to home and, for the first time, I put my hands in the pockets. How deep they were and how warm; it would be a good coat for the long walk to school.

The sparkling of snow made the old barn, which had never felt the slapping stroke of a paint brush, loom in competition with the black bare trunks of trees. The only light came from the stars and the oil lamps of home. I felt loved! But in my vision the red coat, vivid as holly berries, kept haunting me by floating in and out among the pines.

The moonlight framed my Mama standing in the doorway. I threw back my sagging shoulders and waved but I knew, oh, I really knew, she wasn't pleased with that coat. Being a wise and understanding woman, she talked only about the party.

Several weeks later I found, on my bed, a big box. In it was a beautiful sky blue coat of wool, nipped in the waist, with silver buttons going right up to my chin and a stand-up collar.

I looked around and saw Mama standing at the door. "Do you like it?"she asked anxiously. "I love it – I love it – but can we afford something so beautiful?" She told me my father gave her money at Christmas for something special. "What," she asked, "is more special than a thirteen year-old daughter?" "A 38 year-old mother," I said softly, giving her a big kiss and my special bear hug. Other mothers, I thought, may be born, but mine winged her way from heaven.

Alleys

I always enjoyed walking home from high school on a beautiful day. In the spring and fall, when leaves were being added or taken away from the trees on Main Street, you could look west from the summit of the hill and see the clock tower of the courthouse. Happily, Millersburg's school on the top of the hill is still full of children, although it now serves as our grade school.

One fine day I remained after school for a short while and found myself in halls that were rapidly emptying. Alone, I exited through the front doors feeling a strange satisfaction in the absence of other students spilling out beside me. I paused for a moment enjoying a bit of solitude; a rare occurrence for a fifteen year old with three siblings. A familiar voice called to me from an open window, "Where do you suppose that street goes?" It was Miss Moore, my Latin teacher, inclining her head towards the direction she intended.

I followed her gaze across the road, "Oh, that's just an old alley."

"Aren't you curious as to where it goes? Curiosity makes life interesting and you should never underestimate the charm of what you call 'an alley'—they are all so different." She waved good-bye and I continued on my walk.

I took the bait and decided to go home by way of the alley. How could I live in such a small town and never have thought to find where it went? Embarking on a nice walk with a new view of side yards and back yards, I found the alley ended on Route 241 heading northeast out of town. From there I followed two other alleys and ended back out on Main Street. Little did I know then that the houses I passed would be home to people that would become dear to me in my future. The little girl I noticed swinging in her yard would, twelve years hence, become a wonderful babysitter for my own children. The woman sweeping the front porch of the brick house would become a dear, older friend in my adult life, and the large bittersweet-colored Victorian brick home would be lovingly occupied and tended by my grandson and his family.

The weekend came and on the Sunday afternoon following my conversation with Miss Moore, I called a friend and said, "Let's explore alleys." She was eager – nothing else to do. We took our cameras and crisscrossed alleys all over town. The alleys of my youth were never paved, were dusty or muddy, and had no trees and no lights. One alley ended in a wood. Others ended at small old barns weathered silvery gray. It was a day of mystery and we were worn out. Why all these alleys?

Some years before, I had walked along a dusty country street with my cousin. On our way to her home we came to a familiar fork and had the choice of an abandoned alley or a newer road. We always chose the alley—it was shaded and spooky. There was nothing to be afraid of in those days and we would scream and growl like animals, flitting in and out of the shadows, feeling the coolness without the sunshine.

We always considered the commonly tread path that went down to our home in Nashville an alley. It was narrow with a path worn from wheels, first from the wagon pulled by horses Duke and Mollie and later by our first automobile. Grass grew in the middle. It dead-ended in a heap of tall grasses. It was the sled-riding hill of our town. My brother made a bobsled and Mama said we made so much noise when we flew by the living room window that it distracted her piano pupils.

Since those days I have seen narrow streets sided by brick walls (I still call them alleys – much more of a ring to it), alleys paved with brick, some with cobblestones, and others where tall hibiscus hedges screened out the modern world. I walked down an alley that wove behind an Inn where Hawthorne once stayed.

I have seen many movies where alleys formed the plot—twilight came early, a black cat runs from the shadows, an eerie shrieking sound comes from a haunted house with cobwebby windows and one dim light. There were alleys people would sneak in and out of because they had no business in being there.

When I thought of writing about alleys, I decided to ride all over Millersburg and retrace my path from those years below. Those alleys are now paved streets with nice homes and yards; the one that ended at a woods now goes straight through. A few old ones are still there and I saw back porches and decks, gardens and an old barn or two. I know now what I didn't consider at fifteen: most of the alleys led to the back part of each property that held the carriages and horses. You arrived by carriage in the front of the house along the street, and your horse and buggy (who was driving—Papa?) trotted around to the back.

Little did Miss Moore know that she aroused in me a curiosity that would keep me pondering and exploring the rest of my life. I have never forgotten her.

Ouija Board

It was the most exciting party of my childhood; a never-to-be-forgotten experience during the short days of December. My school teacher asked my Mama and her brood for an evening Ouija party. She lived in a big house (or so it seemed at the time), right near the square in town.

She opened the door all dressed in a flowing gown the likes of which we had never seen, shawl with fringe, sparkles in her hair, and lots of bracelets. This did not seem like my teacher at all as she waved us into a room of enchantment filled with a heady fragrance. All the curtains were drawn and light from a single lamp cast shadows from behind a large chair in the center of the room.

My teacher greeted us in a deep, unusual voice and then had us sit in smaller chairs facing the big chair. When we were all settled, she placed on her lap the Ouija board—a well known game board with letters and numbers. Unknown to us, she moved a small planchette on metal casters to and fro on top of the board, pointing among the letters and numbers to spell out words. "The spirits are spelling out words," she said, sounding less and less like my teacher. She was so good at it that we fell completely under her spell. When we asked our childish questions, the planchette moved back and forth to form the answers.

Our Mama said in a serious voice, "Where is my husband?" The letters "Lakeland, Florida" were spelled out. Then Mama said, "What is he doing there?"

The reply was spelled out, "plastering."

Mama said, "My, my, how could the spirits know that?"

"Oh, they know everything," Miss Williamson replied.

After an hour of similar amazing messages, Miss Williamson, remaining in character, served cake with whipped cream. "Pleasseee cheeldren, enjoy yourrr cake and do not be afraid to ask for morrrrrre," she said, her r's rolling.

On the way home, snow just beginning to cover the ground, we walked along the dirt footpath at the edge of town. We huddled as close together as we could to benefit from the light of the lantern held by brother John. Babbling incessantly we peppered our Mama with questions. "Why don't we have an Ouija board?" said nine year old John, "It would be very helpful on my lap during a test at school."

"I couldn't say," countered Mama, "I don't know how to talk with the spirits."

Starting down the hill towards home, snow fell in ever larger flakes. John, in his excitement began swinging the lantern. Mama, carrying three-year-old Helen, instructed him to stop just as Francie fell into the ditch. "Whoa!" Francie said, "A bad spirit shoved me into the ditch but a good spirit helped me out!"

For the next few days, whether things went right or wrong, it was because of "the spirits." A good spirit told me it was not my turn to dry the dishes or told John he didn't have to feed the chickens because they weren't hungry. Mama finally had enough of our nonsense and sat us down at the table. "Now, this is how that board really works…" Pooh! We didn't want to believe a word of it—we were having too much fun.

On the final Sunday of the Christmas holiday, we were invited up the hill to town to have Sunday dinner at Grandma Fisher's. Aunt Mat and Uncle Will joined us and we spent the day together. Since Grandma lived along Main Street, Mama allowed us to bundle up and go outside for a ride on the sled. Francie, Helen and I all managed to fit on that little sled while John, huffing and puffing, pulled us up to the square. As we passed Miss Williamson's house she tapped on the window and motioned for us to come inside. I was concerned, "Should we go in there without Mama?"

"You bet," Francie decided, and in we went to the house of mystery. When Miss Williamson opened the door we were quite disappointed. She looked just like she did when she taught school. She ushered us into the living room where we were dismayed to find a normal room with normal furniture. No big chair and no big shadows. She brought out the Ouija board and explained that she and Mama had decided we should understand how it works. John crossed his arms and looked skeptical. After she described how much she enjoyed making her costume for the party and acting a "part" for us, we told her how wonderful the evening was. We agreed to forget about spirits. Begrudgingly. We lined up to go out the door. I looked back once – hoping to see a gypsy lady and shadows from a lamp. No such luck.

Time to go back to Grandma's to pick up Mama for the walk home. "Aunt Mat" I said, "Do you believe in spirits?"

"Yes," she winked, "but only if they're good ones."

The English Paper

Mr. Fred Almendinger taught at Millersburg High School and was also a noted historian. In his sophomore class during the late 1920's he required us to choose a topic of historical significance and compose an essay. I chose to write a descriptive piece on the French Revolution (1790-1799). Using my imagination, which at sixteen included a flowery array of romantic notions, I wrote twenty-six pages of historical drama in flowery story-telling style. "Give wings to your memory, dear friends, and go back with me to the beautiful country of France where people lived in terror of the king and war was predominant over everything. Forget the trials of today and learn about the cruelty and wickedness of the French Revolution."

Continue reading aloud and in a dramatic voice: "What is that sound I hear—like an extremely loud rumble of thunder? Ah, it is the rush of the whole court, pushing and shoving to salute the new sovereigns, Louis XVI and Marie Antoinette. Let us hurry and try to get a glimpse of them before they enter the castle. The king is short, fat, dull and unattractive. Marie is a treat for the eyes. A beautiful society butterfly who knows only the intimate crowd in which she moves. But the masses do not like their selfish new queen who walks like a goddess of beauty caring not at all for the future of her people."

My ending (strike an anguished pose and place the back of your hand across your furrowed brow): "We have now trampled over bloody streets; we have stumbled over wounded bodies; we have heard the glad shouts and cries of the people as they welcomed a returning hero and also, we have heard the wails of the dying, the boom, boom of the cannon intermingled with the rumble of the death cart. It has been a sad journey and we can only hope that America, land of the free and home of the brave, will never see a war like the French Revolution."

Mr. Almendinger gave me an "A" and wrote on my paper, "This is an excellent paper—it is original and the language is all your own." I have kept those pages all these years and still feel the encouragement of that motivating teacher. Four years earlier, another English teacher had a different opinion: he did not like my writing. All students were to read a chapter in our book and then write from memory what we had read. Example: "The weary man walked the country road, never seeing the fields of corn on either side." My version: "A weary man slowly walked the dusty country road, heaving a great sigh, his eyes downcast, not seeing rows of growing corn where stalks were standing like sentinels." I thought I had made it more interesting but he gave me a D because I added my opinion. I did not like that teacher.

Valentino is Dead

Francie and I, being the two oldest girls in our family and close in age, loved it when Aunt Mat invited us to her home in Akron. Although we loved our life at home, it was very romantic to drive with her in her big car to the city where there were movie houses and wonderful stores with clothing that was neither handed down nor sewn at home. At ages thirteen and eleven, we had colorful imaginations and loved talking about our favorite silent movie stars. Maybe we'd see one in Akron, Ohio!

On a beautiful afternoon we sat together on the big porch swing on the long and wide veranda. The paper boy came by, said a polite hello and tossed us the paper. The headlines screamed out "Rudolph Valentino is dead!" Our idol. Our handsome matinee idol. How could it be?

We walked across the avenue to the lovely park, our arms around one another, tears streaming unchecked down our young cheeks. Our vacation, we agreed, is surely ruined. Between sobs, we agreed to sob for days and days. We lamented his thick black hair, his stylish clothes, his dear face—oh it was just too heartbreaking! Forgetful of the time, we sat in the shade of large maple trees with branches seeming to brood down over us. We knew so little of tragedy.

Returning to Aunt Mat's, we began to cross the street, heads down, still inconsolable. "Girls! The streetcar is coming!" she screamed. We jumped out of harm's way and made our way solemnly up the sidewalk. Hands on hips, standing on the top porch step, our Aunt scolded us for taking leave of her front porch without permission. Upon noticing our tear-stained faces she exclaimed, "Whatever is the matter?" She listened to our sad news and then said, "That's the silliest thing I ever heard of—crying over a movie star. I hope you never have anything to *really* cry about." She turned around and walked back into the house, her back as straight as the posts holding the clothesline.

We plopped ourselves back down on the porch swing. Well, I never! Aunt Mat didn't understand at all. I wanted to go home. Francie started to cry again. Thoughts of our tall, slender Mama with her easy laugh and soothing voice made me begin crying again, too. Holmes County was so far away. Well, Aunt Mat, with two married daughters out of the house and her live-in maid, just didn't have enough to do with her time…that was it. Keeping busy was our Mama's strategy for happiness. Maybe our Aunt Mat just wasn't a happy woman.

The screen door opened. There stood Aunt Mat, her naturally curly hair all out of control despite being pulled back in a bun. She wore white gloves and had her big black purse on her arm. "Come my girls, freshen up because we are going to take the streetcar downtown to O'Neil's Department Store and get you new dresses. Then, we shall have chocolate sundaes." Oh, our Aunt Mat knew just how to solve a problem!

Returning from our shopping trip that evening, we were as happy as a pair of cooing doves, and our Aunt was now, in our minds, a fairy godmother. Our new dresses, both with narrow white lace at the neckline and tiny tucks in the bodice were just right for church. We were sure that if we went to school in the city, they would be just right for that, too. Oh, just wait until our friends at home had a look at those store-bought dresses. We decided that we wouldn't cry any more about Rudolph Valentino until bed time.

The Candy Dish

When Grandma Brown died in 1910, my Grandpa decided to travel west for two reasons: he loved the mountains and he thought the pure air would be good for his asthma. He spent six months to a year in each of many wonderful states and finally settled in Denver, where he died in 1920 at the Hotel Windsor. It had been a friendly evening in the hotel lobby, but Grandpa grew weary, retired early and at age 80, slept his way into the arms of Grandma.

During those years, Grandpa came back to Holmes County each spring to see his five children and many grandchildren. A favorite stop was to see the orchards in bloom on the home farm, now tended lovingly by son, Walter. The house still stands northwest of Nashville, Ohio.

Our family lived across the street from the grocery store and Grandpa, after telling stories of the west, so very far away, would walk us across the street to buy candy. We always wanted chocolates but he would say, "Chocolates are not good for children," and instead bought round pink lozenges. Arriving back home Mama, winking slyly at brother John and me, would say, "Did you thank Grandpa for the candy?"

I can still taste that candy. It all went by like a dream—like eating sweet, pink candy on a summer afternoon, nothing really lasts very long.

✳

The Changes that Come

It will soon be time to fill the car trunk with your favorite plants and flowers and head for the graves of loved ones. During my childhood, we filled sprinkling cans for Mama and then played hide-n-seek among the trees and tombstones.

Many years later, Mother and I were still going together to plant old and new graves – the children, now playing, were mine. In the first spring after an aunt died, the weather was hot and dry; Mom watched me trying to dig holes in the hard ground. "You know," she said, "there are too many relatives who have died and too few of us left to do the planting. The time will come when you must decide which to leave alone."

About four years later I allowed the groundcover to take over Grandma's grave. I couldn't dig a hole big enough for a marigold. You honestly felt like the tombstone was spreading beneath the earth. Mother, in her practical way, remarked, "It's difficult enough to plant graves you still cry over; your dad says a head of lettuce on his grave will do—I want one dogwood and face me towards Nashville's meadows and hills." Age-old hemlocks sighed.

We could laugh at these remarks because we had been given years without sadness. Spring was everywhere—the fields smiled, the birds sang, and old tombstones had not reached the sagging stage. It all looked so beautiful as we left the front gate for the highway.

Years passed by; my in-laws were gone and my own parents rested beneath the ground. Four different times my husband and I planted a dogwood tree on Mom's grave, but none survived (sorry, Papa, no lettuce bed). It all became too much and we had the late Luther Martin, beloved custodian of Oak Hill Cemetery, and his wife, Anna, plant the graves of my husband's relatives.

Now my husband is gone and a grandson and I work together. I realize more and more the meaning of my mother's words, that somewhere along the way, generations must rest in peace, without flower beds.

New Memorial Day approaches and the cemetery becomes fresh, clean, sweet-smelling. Early on that special day, while the town still sleeps, it can be the most peaceful, lovely place around. All those geraniums planted because it makes us feel good to have done something. Tombstones are memorials – they are there as a tribute and so that we shall not lose track of our ancestors. But memorials aren't nearly as pleasant as memories.

Once again, I shall marvel that this large, sleeping area is so carefully mowed and I shall notice graves unplanted. "The time will come…," my mother said. The birds flit from tree to tree— how nice they fly back each spring chirping their bird songs; but another year has flown too and it will not be back.

Reflecting on Grief's Meaning

It is not what you have lost, but what you left that counts.

-- Harold Russell

I've lost my sister, the "baby" of the family. Once again, I take to the country hills and winding roads of Holmes County. I ride slowly—thinking and weeping; grateful for the lack of traffic.

I drive between fields of corn so close to the road, I seem to be trespassing. I pause on a bridge and watch clear water flow gently over smooth stones and being the oldest family survivor, I feel vulnerable. The water flows gently beneath the bridge and finds its way through a meadow, taking with it some of my pain. How neat the countryside, how fresh the smells. Twilight falls and I head the car for home.

Later, I feel sad that obituaries must be so short. "Helen Fisher Martin died in the hospital following a long illness." One is given the impression she was there for weeks on end. Not so. During her last illness, she was cared for in her home by the entire family working together. Daughter Beth brightened her days with flowers, and in June, daughter Connie and husband came took her to their home in Port Huron, Michigan with a view of the St. Clair River.

After staying two months, Helen's condition worsened and at her request, they brought her home and she was taken immediately to the hospital where she required the skilled, compassionate attention of nurses. Her daughter Cris and I decorated her room with quilts, pillows, her favorite chair and photos. Grandson Rhett, eight years old and with solemn purpose, wheeled his Grandma up and down the hall, while Granddaughter Alathea walked along beside and held her Grandma's hand. "My beauties" Helen would call them. Husband Barney combed her hair. She was there for four days charming the staff and holding court as friends and family came and went. Gradually, she wore out and her daughter, Cris, and I settled in to hold vigil, speaking softly, providing reassurances. Cris sang to her off and on all night; snippets of old movies, Helen's Judy Garland favorites. At one point, we were heartened to observe her quite lucidly speaking to my late husband. I noticed that their conversation took place at the same time of day, to the minute, that my husband had departed this earth. We took comfort, believing that he was there to help her make her transition. We remained with her all night, and the next morning, as we sipped tea together at her bedside, she ceased to breathe.

Yes, an obituary is a cold methodical way of informing the community it has lost another citizen. In many corners of each neighborhood, there is sadness, and that person who kindles the slow-dying embers of hope within our souls, is, to each of us, at that agonizing time, the most important person on this earth.

My sister enjoyed the poem, *Ritual*, by Jane Merchant —"She sips her coffee, and she goes - undaunted by life's harshest blows; and she has borne them all." She relished the columns I wrote about civic action in the community and always knew when I didn't write exactly the way I felt and would say, "Whose toes were you afraid of stepping on when you wrote that?"

I shall have trouble swallowing my morning coffee for some weeks to come—"My sister knows there is no ill - so dire a cup of coffee will - not help to soothe its pain. A cup of coffee, hot and black - is balm for any loss or lack - is ease for any strain."

So now, dear Helen, with a lump in my throat and tears in my eyes, I drink this steaming brew for you and recall, when you were twenty-one, a Cleveland doctor told you personally you might live a couple more years and not to have any children. You showed them. You lived to be sixty-nine even though it was rough, and you had three lovely daughters. Perhaps, and let's laugh together as of yore-it was the coffee.

The Kitchen Table

As a child, I had done my homework at the big, long kitchen table of wood that held three oil lamps. What joys and trials that table has borne. Many relatives ate impromptu meals there as we went up and down the cellar stairs, choosing from rows and rows of fruits and vegetables stored there in the cool damp. Each autumn, our teachers were invited for dinner when pumpkin pies were plentiful and it was easier to kill and dress a couple of chickens while the weather held off. We ate all our meals at that table. There was no dining room with "company" furniture.

It was at that kitchen table that Doc Elder found us when he came to tell Mama, in his kind, soft voice, that her father had died. The operator who received the call in her little telephone office decided it would be better to tell the doctor instead of our Mama, who was expecting her sixth child and had not been well. It was the first time I ever saw our Mama cry and we were frightened. She slowly lowered her head to the table and sobbed. I wouldn't see her cry again until the last of her babies died at age two. The table at that time was covered with oil-cloth upon which she cradled her weeping face in folded arms.

Mama's older sister Alda sat at the table sewing lace on dresses for my sister and me to wear on Children's Day for our vocal duet. As we fought over which dress would be finished first, Aunt Alda sent us outside to pick her a bouquet of wildflowers and when that task was completed, told us to "Get out of the kitchen and stay out!"

During the winter when my sister was quarantined off the kitchen with scarlet fever, the rest of us studied at the table and spoke softly. As she grew stronger, my brother and I would yell back and forth to her, however, she took a turn for the worse again and we were sent to the living room to study—the only time we took that task away from the table and the oil lamps.

Mama's friend Charley came to the table when he returned from World War I and wore his uniform to supper. He looked wonderful, but refused to play ball with us after dinner and walked quietly home. Mama told us, "He is still fighting the war in his heart." How could he be so sick and look so well?

Decisions were made at that table, punishments meted out, praise given, news shared. Dress patterns were laid out there; and clothes folded smelling fresh from hanging on the clothes line in the sun. Pies cooled, buckets of peas waited to be shelled, bushel baskets of apples and a poke filled with red, yellow, and green peppers brought color and garden fragrance. After supper, sheets of piano music spread out waiting to be chosen for just the right pupil lay crisply as Mama walked back and forth with a finger on her chin; allegro or andante…a march or a waltz…who would play them?

When, as a teenager my best friend came into our house for a visit wearing…bright…red…lipstick, one look on my Mama's face peering up above her spectacles as she mended clothes was enough to send that friend packing. After she left, I was called to the table and told to find another friend. I cried myself to sleep but to Mama's credit she decided to take me to the drug store in Millersburg where she picked out a soft pink color that I would be permitted to wear on special occasions.

Yes, the kitchen table was my favorite place during my growing up years. Later, it would reign supreme in my own family with heated conversations after a certain sports event. I would stand at the counter making peanut butter and bacon sandwiches and keep my opinions to myself, thinking instead of my Mama and Papa sitting at the table in the chilly evenings, their faces softly lit by the oil lamps, murmuring softly, wafting a sense of peace through our home like scent.

The Place

"The Place" has become a sanctuary of peace in later life. On a summer's day in 1927, a conversation occurred between my father and Uncle Commodore DeWitt that changed our lives forever. My uncle, a chef, wanted to start a restaurant in Millersburg with Papa (a plasterer by trade) as manager and co-owner, and Papa agreed.

Everything was sold except the twenty-three acres called the "Place" which was left undisturbed for five or six years because of our busy lives. But a day finally came when Papa and brother John had time to tramp the woodsy acreage. When they returned John said to me, "Gee sis, it's beautiful out there—the dogwoods are bright red, the maples pure gold and the woods, so dense."

Time had the wings of an eagle and it was in my first year of marriage that I returned to the Place with Papa (Mama, a classical pianist was busy giving piano lessons). I parked in a field expecting easy access to the woods, but a thicket of blackberry bushes, facing south, formed an impenetrable hedge. We walked toward the road and found an opening into a shaded area where we discovered a magnificent bed of ferns. (Years later, when I saw a fern grotto in Hawaii, I thought of the Place.) We also came upon a large area of ground pine which, to Papa's amusement, I walked around even though he said footsteps would not harm it.

The shed, of course, was long gone—could some boards still be rotting down deep in the underbrush? Nature had, years ago, taken care of the small coal mine and it was now a low place between two ridges and completely covered with a growth of wild things.

The seasons passed, one after the other, and I was busy rearing my family of three. In 1941, when the youngest was one year old, my brother, John, (at age 31) and his wife were killed in an automobile accident leaving behind two little girls, Pat and Betty, who were then raised by a maternal aunt and her husband. This was devastating for all of us. Aunt Alda came to comfort Mama and one day my husband took my father to the Place where he wished to be left alone. He was found later, sitting on a log, patched with moss, crying. Somehow my parents survived, as all parents do, in a time of tragedy.

In 1947, the restaurant was sold. My life was busy and it was good that Dad had friends to take him to his wooded lot. Some years later, the next family member to go to the Place was my son John, named for my brother. He and his grandpa walked the woods until they came to the stone wall that had been made back in World War I, when an area was cleared for crops. The last time Dad tramped the special area was in the early spring of the 1960's when he and my husband went hunting for mushrooms.

In March of 1965 my mother died at age 84. In May Papa asked me to take him to the Place. As we neared the front of the woodlands he sighed, "Stop here—I can't walk in today." We were sitting there in silence peering through the trees to see the dogwood blossoms when he said, "I saw a lawyer today and I have willed you the woods." He was elated at my surprise. He died September 1965 at age 83.

The next time I visited my haven I was with grandsons, Mike and Eric, (my husband died in 1977) to dig dogwoods. They did not realize that memories were swirling around me or that I stared into space seeing things they could not see and hearing voices that did not exist.

Now, it has been years since I have been back—so why do I keep the Place? Quite simply, because it is there and it is important to me. The trees have healed many wounds and given spiritual growth when it was needed. I hear joyous laughter and a little red wagon going bumpity-bump-bump over exposed tree roots. It has often occurred to me that I do not feel my age when my mind is occupied with nature.

After the years have passed, it's the sensations I remember most of childhood. Cold toes in a pair of snow boots, or the feel of a new store-bought coat. Or sometimes the sweet taste of ice cream on Saturday night. The Place brings it all back to me. Twenty-three acres–a sanctuary of peace–that my Mama called the "Place." This is where it all rests.

The Sun on the Hill

If you've lived long enough, you will, sooner or later, agonize over the loss of a loved one. It's unavoidable. Many people have asked how long my husband has been gone—do I still miss him—when did I start feeling like a human being again?" They need support and want to be told their similar feelings of grief are normal, but I am a private person and such personal notions were too painful to write about. I have attempted to write about it. Now and then, I touched on the edges of my anguish, but like a bird learning to fly, was hesitant to leave my nest. I would circle around my sorrow as lace circles the edges of an old handkerchief. Once, I raced through the center of my loneliness, writing a few sentences, then stopping quickly, trembling like a frightened deer, when, after venturing into the lights, leaps quickly back to the woods, safe from prying eyes.

My husband died over thirty years ago and I shall always miss him but now I don't sit and deliberately think about him or I would still cry. Until I was able to accept the difficult fact that he was really gone I was nearly wild with grief. Surely he would walk through the door, come down the stairs and laugh and joke with me and I would have so much to tell him. I would "see" him in a crowd and that jolt would be followed by acute sorrow and stabbing pain.

For weeks I felt there should be something I could do that would bring him back. This caused a desolate feeling of hopelessness. I felt abandoned—half a person. It took all the determination, courage, and self-discipline I could muster to get through this period in one piece. The strong desire to be independent and manage my own affairs helped immeasurably.

Grief is so complex, so filled with a variety of emotions that, for a time, it changed my personality, which baffled my friends. No two people grieve alike and none recovers in the same period of time. I was grateful my children gave no advice, listened to my rambling and never asked more of me than I could give.

Acquaintances are not always kind—one person said, "Don't you think it's time you face reality?" This cruel remark was made when three months had passed by a person who has never experienced a similar loss. The insensitivity of some individuals during a crisis in not easily forgotten. You can only endure.

Some people have delayed grief. Mine started immediately. I cried for weeks on end. There were no mornings, no nights, no days, no sun, and no rain—just tears. I cried in every room in the house; I cried on my flowers, the bushes I trimmed, the furniture I dusted. I nearly went berserk when I did my first wash with only my garments swishing around. I cried in all kinds of places—on the floor, every bed, in the wardrobe, with my head on the kitchen table, during a bath. I cried out in the woods behind our home where we took so many walks together and once hid under a big, old hemlock tree so that my grandchildren who had come to look for me would not see my haggard, tear-blotched face. I cried until I slept from emotional exhaustion. My world was one of constant moisture. Having once suffered through the tragedy of my brother's death unable to cry, I was grateful for tears. They helped me to get well.

It wasn't until the second week I realized I was a widow. The word had always terrified me; I was distraught, yelling out in the middle of the night, "No, no, no!" I was terribly scared. There was nothing but emptiness and numbing loneliness in my life. I feared I couldn't make it and would forever be shackled to despair.

I knew it was best to keep busy—it was the only way, but oh, how difficult when you are dead tired from lack of rest. Getting to sleep was like trying to catch a butterfly—I would almost drift off only to be wide awake again. During that time I lost weight and dropped to 80 pounds from my normal 120. The food my children brought me wouldn't stay down. I got over this—I had to. I looked twenty years older and still had some pride.

I had no desire for a social life which only intensified my "aloneness." Consolation was derived from my family and writing letters to long-standing friends seldom seen. I took many rides alone in the car, eating in different towns. Strangers were wonderful therapy for me. I eventually dropped the "Mrs." from my name and began using my given name. This was very strange to a woman married prior to 1950.

Don't offer advice to a grieving person. Please don't say, "Count your blessings." Why was my heart not wise enough to know I was blessed? You feel guilty because you can't cope. Don't add to the burden. There was a deplorable time when, had I been told birds never sing, I would have nodded my head in agreement. I had a sodden spirit.

The advice "give it a year" caused an illusionary feeling that a magic wand would wave over me and all would be well. I made myself take a couple of nice bus tour trips and was beginning to accept some of the devastating change, but at the end of the year I called a friend fifteen years my senior. Sobbing, I asked her why I was still being ripped apart inside. "My dear," she replied, "It takes much longer than a year. Live each day the best you can and quit trying to hurry recovery because it can't be done. One day you will suddenly feel in control of your life again."

It happened to me on the top of my hill. I often went there to watch the sunset and on summer mornings I would also walk there to watch the sun rise. I never cried on my hill, but in that small clearing surrounded by pines and wild things, I said my prayers. It was a sunny mid-afternoon in November the next year, about eighteen months after my husband had gone. I was dreading the approaching holidays when I noticed a young pine had grown—it was fresh and pretty and would soon feel the softness of snowflakes.

Suddenly, everything was different—I had weathered the storm. In November I felt like Spring—lilacs and apple blossoms. Dear God, I was going to make it. I knew, even though my eyes stayed dry, my heart would still cry, but now I could handle it. I would survive. As Albert Camus wrote, "In the midst of winter, I finally learned that in me was an invincible summer."

Those of you who have yet to suffer may think I have exaggerated—that you would cope much better than I. That could be but don't be too sure. Just remember, you do survive and are a stronger, more compassionate person because of what you've been through. Those of you who have suffered or continue to suffer realize that I have not told all; that like a rose just starting to bloom, I have opened for now, only a few petals. Now, several years later, I am reminding what my Mother, who suffered many tragedies and always regained her cheerfulness said, "Every sadness leaves a scar on the heart that never completely heals, but it's so amazing, so wonderful how you learn to accept them and be happy again. It's what God expects us to do."

✳

Epilogue

An Age Old Subject

If I had my way, we would never grow old – and sunshine I'd bring every day – if I had my way...from a song by Lou Klein in 1913 and recorded by the Mills Brothers and Bing Crosby in the 1930's.

Our country faces what might be called an epidemic of aging. The news media is constantly writing or talking about aging citizens so I may as well have a fling at it. You are being told what to do and what not to do, how to age gracefully, etc. I think the only way to reach your dotage (ghastly word) is to forget about it except when your doctor, lawyer, or the Federal Government forces you to admit cumulative years. As my son, Richard, told me, "It isn't how old you get, but how you get old." I wrote this article first in the 1970s. Now at age ninety-eight I find the subject even more apropos.

My generation of peers born between 1900 and 1920 are called the General Issue (GI) or Hero Generation. We have been described as having the general attitude of conformity; we must all agree, all work the same way, and all look the same. We have shared the characteristics of gallantry and civic mindedness under firm leadership. We didn't like wimps, whiners, and slackers. There are few of us left. Most of the famous GI-ers are gone: John F Kennedy, Winston Churchill, and Mother Teresa. We grew up in big families where men were strong and women fainted from time to time. We were the world's first teenagers; in fact, it was a term that was specifically invented for us. Our professional careers began in the time of the great depression and we regarded work as a privilege and a gift. Because we worked when work was scarce, we believe that you should stick to your job and be loyal to your employer. That's why we can't understand how people can walk away from a job.

There are so many interpretations of age; it's no wonder countless books are written on the subject. From a young person's point of view, a woman of forty may remind them of fall when beautiful leaves suddenly wing their way downward. To a woman of 60 she is springtime when all the trees are bursting with life. I once heard a woman of 85 say to my 70 year-old mother, "But you are still quite young."

As long as I can play hide and seek, my great-nephew, Rhett, will think of me as being young. One day when I said I was too old for that sort of thing, he cried, "You are not old – you're not, you're not." To alleviate his fears I was about to cave in, I played the game so well he thought I was lost!

Clara Booth Luce, who was married to the late Henry R. Luce of Time, Inc., was quoted as saying after her husband died, "I was building a house in Hawaii, where I was going to do nothing but look at the ocean, having led such an active life, and then gradually it began to dawn on me that I would either fill my remaining years with intellectual relationships (at age 80 she has returned to political life) and work or I would wither away." When asked if she worried about old age, she replied, "My old friend, Bernard Baruch, used to say as he grew older, "I consider the alternative and resign myself.""

Godfrey Holloway, in his delightful booklet, "The Empress," has an unusual approach in describing the difference between that beautiful, ancient hotel in Victoria, B.C. and the modern hotel of today. He tells us that a bright, young girl with her modish dress and modern ideas will attract attention but get a roomful and there is a depressing similarity.

"Introduce an older woman into such a crowd. One who is alive and eager. It is obvious that experience counts, that beauty cared for beyond the first flush of youth is the more alluring beauty, that—well, sophistication and good manners and a real knowledge of how the world works, enable such a woman to meet and overwhelm without effort the frantic yet basically identical competition of the young. Add to this the mature ability to be a little bit different and you have a woman with whom the young crowd cannot compete."

Not everyone will agree but don't you find the words encouraging? The older woman is not a frump, but an attractive, interesting human being. However, I do not feel like the writer who said, "What shall I do in the future? Bring me the tea leaves please." I live my life in the present.

Today is now and it is mine—you can have tomorrow, and yet, perhaps...I'll take just one more tea leaf?

Photo List

Figure 1   Miss Effie Brown. There were several lovely portraits of Effie that were taken during her teenage years. This one was likely taken to celebrate her graduation from the Ashland School of Music. The lace on her blouse would have been crocheted by her mother.

Figure 2   Siblings (from left) John, Francie, and Alathea on the porch in Akron, Ohio about 1915.

Figure 3   Mr. Herbert Fisher looking quite dapper. I love the look on his face – he knows how good looking he is. This was taken prior to marrying Effie.

Figure 4   Alathea, Mama's helper. Taken about age 11.

Figure 5   Sister Francie at about 8 years old. No smile for the camera. We have another picture from the same sitting with Francie wearing glasses. You can tell she was none too pleased at having to be sitting in front of the camera.

Figure 6   Sister Helen at about age 12.

Figure 7   A very young brother John Lee Fisher with short pants, black knee high hose, and his little hat.

Figure 8   Papa (on left) and the disbelieving car salesmen who taught him to drive before he left the lot.

Figure 9   Mama holding our dear little sister Amy prior to her death later that year. This picture is a favorite because it shows our beautiful mother with her strong hands and the lovely braid she always wore wrapped around her head. Younger sister Helen stands beside her.

Figure 10   Beloved teacher Miss Bell who "sent me up to 4th grade". Alathea (blonde hair) right beside her.

Figure 11   Brother John and his first good friend and next door neighbor, Bidge Nevin.

Figure 12   John Lee Fisher, 16 years old.

Figure 13   Grandpa and Grandma Fisher in the year before he died. I love this picture because of Grandpa's handle bar moustache which I could always reach up and pull on. They are standing in front of his beloved garden.

Figure 14   Aunt Mat and Uncle Will Ridge. I included this picture because Aunt Mat was in so many of the stories. This portrait captures her kindness coupled with her "no nonsense" attitude.

Figure 15   Grandpa and Grandma (Fanny) Fisher standing in a fallow field.

Figure 16   The family ready for Saturday night about 1919: Papa, Alathea, John, Francie, and Mama holding baby Helen. This was after Helen had to learn to walk again following her long illness. Mama crocheted (tatted) the lace trim on the front of her apron.

Figure 17   John Van Buren Fisher (Grandpa), a formal tradesman picture as a plasterer of walls.

Figure 18   A photo of brother John and Mama. I included this picture for several reasons, 1) because of the vulnerability of my mother's smile, 2) the confidence and youth of my brother, 3) the obvious love between the two of them, and 4) my mother's changing wardrobe as the decades passed. His death would change our lives.

Figure 19   Alathea during high school. Fur stoles were all the rage.

Figure 20   Helen a few years older, more confident now (of course a fur stole).

Figure 21   Sister Francie at 18. Francie, Helen and I were known as the "Three Beautiful Fisher Sisters"

Figure 22   A picture of Alathea at 20 in 1921. A very stylish flapper.

Figure 23   Picnic at the Place. Note Papa in his miner's cap standing between Aunt Laurie and Mama. Papa was very protective of Mama that day because she had arrived at The Place trying to smile bravely. My parents were still grieving noticeably after my little sister Amy's death.

Figure 24   A loving photo of Mama and Papa, in their eighties. My father surprised my mother at the last minute before this photo was taken. This tenderness characterized their relationship.

Figure 25   The author, Alathea Fisher Maxwell, Christmas Day 2009.

www.ingramcontent.com/pod-product-compliance
Lightning Source LLC
LaVergne TN
LVHW091153080426
835509LV00006B/663